W9-CDI-360

GRAND CANYON

NATIONAL PARK

ADVENTURE, EXPLORE, DISCOVER

DOREEN GONZALES

MyReportLinks.com Books
an imprint of
Enslow Publishers, Inc. **E**
Box 398, 40 Industrial Road
Berkeley Heights, NJ 07922
USA

MyReportLinks.com Books, an imprint of Enslow Publishers, Inc. MyReportLinks®
is a registered trademark of Enslow Publishers, Inc.

Library of Congress Cataloging-in-Publication Data

Gonzales, Doreen.
  Grand Canyon National Park : adventure, explore, discover / Doreen Gonzales.
      p. cm. — (America's national parks)
  Summary: "A virtual tour of Grand Canyon National Park, with chapters devoted to the
history of this region, history of the park, plant and animal life, environmental problems facing
the park, and activities in the area"—Provided by publisher.
  Includes bibliographical references and index.
  ISBN-13: 978-1-59845-100-9 (hardcover)
  ISBN-10: 1-59845-100-6 (hardcover)
  1. Grand Canyon National Park (Ariz.)—Juvenile literature, 2. Grand Canyon (Ariz.)—Juvenile
literature, I. Title. II. Series.
  F788.G64 2009
  979.1'32—dc22

                                    2007039057

Printed in the United States of America

10 9 8 7 6 5 4 3 2 1

To Our Readers:
Through the purchase of this book, you and your library gain access to the Report Links that specifically back
up this book.
The Publisher will provide access to the Report Links that back up this book and will keep these Report Links
up to date on **www.myreportlinks.com** for five years from the book's first publication date.
We have done our best to make sure all Internet addresses in this book were active and appropriate when we
went to press. However, the author and the Publisher have no control over, and assume no liability for, the material available on those Internet sites or on other Web sites they may link to.
The usage of the MyReportLinks.com Books Web site is subject to the terms and conditions stated on the Usage
Policy Statement on **www.myreportlinks.com**.
A password may be required to access the Report Links that back up this book. The password is found on the
bottom of page 4 of this book.
Any comments or suggestions can be sent by e-mail to comments@myreportlinks.com or to the address on the
back cover.

♻ Enslow Publishers, Inc., is committed to printing our books on recycled paper. The paper in every book contains 10% to 30% post-consumer waste (PCW). The cover board on the outside of each book contains 100%
PCW. Our goal is to do our part to help young people and the environment too!

Photo Credits: APN Media, LLC, p. 58; Arizona Office of Tourism, p. 116; Arizona State Museum, p. 33;
AZNETCO, p. 38; © Bob Ribokas, 1994–2000, pp. 24, 103; DesertUSA.com and Digital West Media, Inc., p. 76;
Falcon Research Group, p. 79; Glen Canyon Institute, p. 94; Grand Canyon Railway, p. 41; Grand Canyon Trust,
p. 88; ITCA, p. 114; Library of Congress, pp. 34, 37; Living Rivers, p. 53; Museum of Northern Arizona, p. 21;
MyReportLinks.com Books, p. 4; National Park Service, pp. 5, 10, 15, 97, 98; Northern Arizona University,
p. 30; NPCA, p. 92; Photos.com, p. 44; Powell Museum, p. 35; Shutterstock.com, pp. 1, 3, 6, 7, 8-9, 11, 13,
18–19, 22, 27, 49, 50, 54, 57, 59, 63, 65, 66, 70, 74, 81, 82, 83, 84, 86–87, 90, 96, 100-101, 106, 110, 113,
and all chapter-openers of electronics; Southwest Media Relations, LLC, p. 104; The Sierra Club, p. 42;
TravelWest.net, p. 108; University of North Texas, p. 32; University of Texas Libraries, p. 47; U.S. Fish & Wildlife
Service, p. 56; Wiley Publishing, Inc., p. 72; Xanterra Parks and Resorts, p. 61.

Cover Photo: Shutterstock.com

CONTENTS

MyReportLinks.com Books
Great Books, Great Links, Great for Research!

The Internet sites featured in this book can save you hours of research time. These Internet sites—we call them **"Report Links"**—are constantly changing, but we keep them up to date on our Web site.

When you see this "Approved Web Site" logo, you will know that we are directing you to a great Internet site that will help you with your research.

Give it a try! Type http://www.myreportlinks.com into your browser, click on the series title and enter the password, then click on the book title, and scroll down to the Report Links listed for this book.

The Report Links will bring you to great source documents, photographs, and illustrations. MyReportLinks.com Books save you time, feature Report Links that are kept up to date, and make report writing easier than ever! A complete listing of the Report Links can be found on pages 118–119 at the back of the book.

Please see "To Our Readers" on the copyright page for important information about this book, the MyReportLinks.com Web site, and the Report Links that back up this book.

Please enter **GCP1684** if asked for a password.

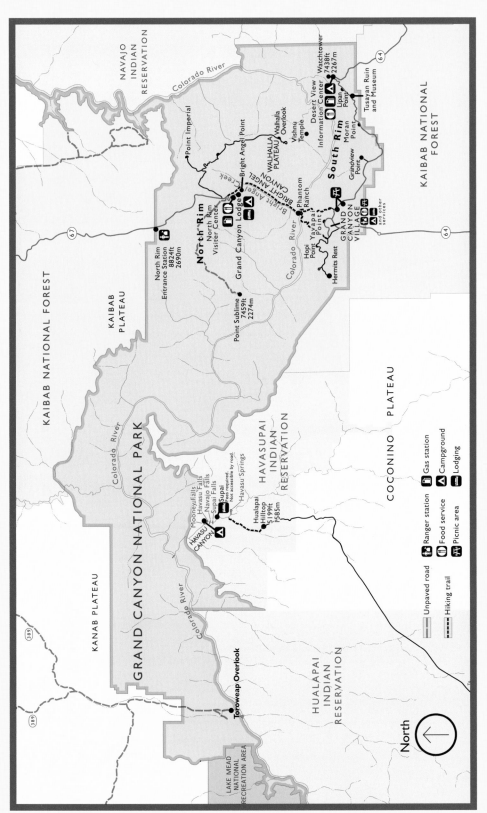

NAVAJO
INDIAN
RESERVATION

Colorado River

KAIBAB NATIONAL
FOREST

64

Watchtower
7438ft
2267m

Desert View
Information Center
Lipan
Point

Tusayan Ruin
and Museum

KAIBAB NATIONAL
FOREST

Point Imperial

Bright Angel Point
Walhalla
Overlook
WALHALLA
PLATEAU

Vishnu
Temple

Moran
Point

South Rim

Bright Angel Creek

North Rim
Visiter Center
North Rim

Grand Canyon Lodge

BRIGHT ANGEL
CANYON

Phantom
Ranch

Grandview
Point

GRAND
CANYON
VILLAGE

and other
services

64

North Rim
Entrance Station
8824ft
2690m

67

Colorado River

Hopi
Point
Yavapai
Point

Point Sublime
7459ft
2274m

Hermits Rest

KAIBAB
PLATEAU

GRAND CANYON NATIONAL PARK

KAIBAB NATIONAL FOREST

Colorado River

COCONINO

PLATEAU

HAVASUPAI
INDIAN
RESERVATION

Mooney Falls
Havasu Falls
Navajo Falls
Supai Falls
Supai

Fees required.
Not accessible by road.
Havasu Springs

Hualapai
Hilltop
5199ft
1585m

HAVASU
CANYON

KANAB PLATEAU

Colorado River

389

389

HUALAPAI
INDIAN
RESERVATION

Toroweap Overlook

LAKE MEAD NATIONAL RECREATION AREA

North

Gas station
Ranger station
Food service
Campground
Lodging
Picnic area

Unpaved road
Hiking trail

▲ Grand Canyon National Park and some of its main points of interest.

🌵 Grand Canyon National Park was established on February 26, 1919. It is located in the northwest corner of Arizona.

🐍 Grand Canyon National Park encompasses 1,904 square miles (4,950 square kilometers). In addition to the Canyon, park boundaries take in high desert plateaus, side canyons, rivers, streams, forests, and cliffs.

🌵 The Grand Canyon is one of the largest canyons in the world. It is 277 river miles (446 kilometers) long and averages ten miles (16 kilometers) wide and one mile (1,609 meters) deep.

🐍 Rocks from the bottom to the top of the Grand Canyon form a discontinuous geologic time line showing almost 2 billion years of the earth's history. The rock formations are an astounding array of reds, oranges, and purples.

🌵 Annual precipitation on the South Rim is sixteen inches (forty-one centimeters). The North Rim receives an average of twenty-five inches (sixty-four centimeters). The Inner Canyon receives only nine inches (twenty-two centimeters).

🐍 Some of the most commonly seen animals in Grand Canyon National Park are elk, mule deer, bats, birds, squirrels, lizards, and snakes.

🌵 The park is home to several endangered or threatened animal species. These include the California condor, humpback chub, Southwestern willow flycatcher, Mexican spotted owl, and desert tortoise. The bald eagle also lives there during the winter, a bird that came off the endangered list in 2007.

- Favorite activities in Grand Canyon National Park include sight-seeing, hiking, river rafting, camping, picnicking, and bicycling.

- South Rim visitor centers include the Desert View Information Center, Tusayan Museum, Canyon View Information Plaza, Yavapai Observation Station, and Kolb Studio. The North Rim Visitor Center is the only National Park Service visitor center on the North Rim. There is, however, a U.S. Forest Service visitor center at Jacob Lake on the North Rim.

- The South Rim is open twenty-four hours a day, every day of the year. Many visitor services are available year-round. The road to the North Rim is often closed from mid-November until mid-May due to snow. Most visitor services on the North Rim are only open from mid-May to mid-October.

- Grand Canyon National Park hosts more than 4 million visitors per year. As of 2009, seven-day admission was $25 per vehicle and can be used on both rims.

- The telephone number for general visitor information is (928) 638-7888.

- The official National Park Service Web site for Grand Canyon National Park is http://www.nps.gov/grca/.

- To request information via mail, write to:
  Grand Canyon National Park
  P.O. Box 129
  Grand Canyon, AZ 86023

Chapter

1

Most visitors to Grand Canyon National Park enter at the South Rim, part of which is shown here.

Mountain Lying Down

There is a enormous hole in the northwest corner of Arizona. Early Americans called it the Big Canon. The Paiute Indians before them called the nearby region the Kaibab Plateau, which means "Mountain Lying Down.[1]" Today we know this giant gorge as the Grand Canyon. The Grand Canyon is a place so spectacular it is considered one of the natural wonders of the world.

→ LOCATION

The Grand Canyon runs east to west across the Colorado Plateau. A plateau is an area of land that is higher than the land around it. Plateaus are flat on top.

The Colorado Plateau stretches across parts of Colorado, Utah, New Mexico, and Arizona. Many canyons break up the plateau. The largest of these is the Grand Canyon. The

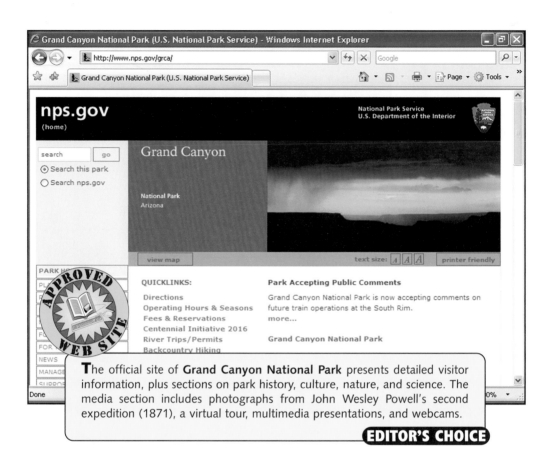

The official site of **Grand Canyon National Park** presents detailed visitor information, plus sections on park history, culture, nature, and science. The media section includes photographs from John Wesley Powell's second expedition (1871), a virtual tour, multimedia presentations, and webcams.

EDITOR'S CHOICE

Grand Canyon stretches from Lees Ferry, Arizona, in the east to Arizona's Grand Wash Cliffs on the west. It is 277 river miles (446 kilometers) long. The gorge averages ten miles (16 kilometers) across and one mile (1,609 meters) deep. The Grand Canyon is so large, in fact, that it can be seen from outer space.

⊖ THE SOUTH RIM

The Grand Canyon has two top edges. They are known as rims. One rim stretches east to west along the south side of the canyon. This is called the South Rim.

The Grand Canyon's South Rim is reached by traveling east from Cameron, Arizona, or north from either Williams or Flagstaff, Arizona. The land here is about 7,000 feet (2,100 meters) above sea level.

Summers on the South Rim are warm, though they are quite cool compared to summer in most of Arizona. Daytime temperatures reach into the 80°s F (30°C). Winter temperatures are cold. The average daytime highs are in the 40°s F (4°C). At night, temperatures can dip into the teens.

The South Rim receives sixteen inches (forty-one centimeters) of precipitation each year. In the summer, this comes as rain. Snow is common in the winter.

Lees Ferry is the point at which the rim of the canyon is almost even with the Colorado River.

→THE NORTH RIM

The land along the north side of the canyon is called the North Rim. The Grand Canyon's North Rim is surrounded by wilderness. Highway 67 from Jacob Lake, Arizona, is the only paved road that leads to the North Rim. The closest towns are about forty-five and seventy-five miles away (72.4 to 120.7 kilometers).

The North Rim is higher than the South Rim. It is more than 8,000 feet (2,400 meters) above sea level. It is also cooler than the South Rim. In the summer, daytime temperatures average in the 70°s F (21°C). Winter temperatures average in the high 30°s F (–1°C).

The North Rim gets about twenty-five inches (sixty-four centimeters) of precipitation a year. Thunderstorms are common in July, August, and September. Winters are snowy. More than ten feet (three meters) of snow falls there on average.[2]

→THE INNER CANYON

The land below the rims is known as the Inner Canyon. At the bottom of the canyon, summer temperatures can exceed 105°F (40°C). In the winter, daytime temperatures average in the 50°s F (10°C). The bottom of the canyon gets only 9.8 inches (24.9 centimeters) of precipitation a year. Less than one inch (two centimeters) of this comes as snow.

Supai, Arizona, is the only town in the Inner Canyon. Supai is in a side canyon (Havasu Canyon) south of the main canyon. It is the capital of the Havasupai Indian Reservation. Supai is eight miles (thirteen kilometers) from the nearest road. The only way to get there is by foot, horse, or helicopter.

The Colorado River lies at the bottom of the Inner Canyon. It is from four thousand to six thousand feet (1,200 to 1,600 meters) below the rim.

➔ THE RIVER

The Colorado River begins high in the mountains of Colorado and flows west. It winds 1,450

The rock layers that can be seen at the ▷ lowest depths of the Grand Canyon were carved out billions of years ago. Each layer tells geologists about the history of the earth at that time.

miles (2,334 kilometers) across the Southwest before emptying into the Gulf of California. Along the way, the river runs through the entire length of the Grand Canyon. The Colorado River averages 40 feet (12 meters) deep and almost 300 feet (91 meters) across.

The Colorado runs right up to the canyon walls in some areas. Beaches line the river in other places. Some beaches lead to side canyons. Creeks flow through some of these canyons to the river. Most of the side canyons have creeks flowing through them only when rain or snow falls. They are dry for much of the year.

At Lees Ferry the canyon's rim and the river are almost even. Then the river drops. Sometimes it drops quickly over a short distance. This increases the water flow in a small area, making rough water known as rapids. Rapids form at the mouth of tributaries where the streams carry rocks into the river. This dams the flow, forcing the river to drop over the dam. All rapids are full of rocks and boulders. The drops and rocks create water that foams and bubbles. This is called white water. The Colorado River has dozens of white-water rapids.

→THE UNIQUE CANYON

The rocks at the bottom of the Grand Canyon are almost 2 billion years old. The ones on top are much newer. They are just 270 million years old.[3]

In between, canyon rocks are stacked in layers according to when they were formed. This makes the Grand Canyon a kind of time line from the bottom to the top.

Each rock layer tells a story about what was happening on earth during a certain period of time. In fact, the canyon is one of the most complete records of geologic history anywhere on the earth. The Grand Canyon, therefore, is a valuable place. Geologists go there to study the earth's natural forces. Still, there are periods as long as a billion years missing from the geologic record. These missing time periods are referred to as unconformities.

The official site of the National Park Service offers video and interactive multimedia features, a park locator map, and educational materials, plus sections on park history, nature, culture, and science. Plan a visit by using the interactive map.

Access this Web site from http://www.myreportlinks.com

Paleontologists also find the Grand Canyon interesting. They study fossils. Fossils from many different time periods have been found in the canyon. Ferns, ancient sea creatures, and even ancient reptile tracks have been preserved in its rocks.

In addition, archaeologists are intrigued by the history of the canyon. These scientists study ancient cultures. Experts have identified more than 4,800 places where prehistoric people lived or traveled near the Grand Canyon. Hundreds of baskets, tools, and rock paintings have been found in and around the canyon. There are even the ruins of some homes. Archaeologists examine these artifacts to learn about how the ancient residents lived.

Finally, biologists study the area. The park is home to many different plants and animals. This gives biologists a living laboratory in which to learn about various species.

⊖ THE CANYON'S BEAUTY

The Grand Canyon is more than a scientific wonder, though. It is one of nature's most spectacular works of art. Layers of different-colored stone reflect the day's changing light in a myriad of reds, pinks, and blues. At sunrise and sunset some rocks seem to glow.

Writers, painters, and photographers have found the canyon to be hypnotic. Many have tried to describe its beauty in pictures and words. Yet even the best artists only come close to capturing its splendor. The Grand Canyon must be seen in person to be fully appreciated.

A NATIONAL PARK

In 1919, President Woodrow Wilson signed a bill that made the Grand Canyon and the area around it a national park. Since then the size of Grand Canyon National Park (GCNP) has increased. Today it covers nearly two thousand square miles (five thousand square kilometers) of land. This makes the park larger than the state of Rhode Island.

But it is not just the people of the United States who find the canyon valuable. In 1979 the park was named a World Heritage Site. This title identifies the Grand Canyon as a place special to our planet. Today people all over the world know there is no other place quite like the Grand Canyon.

Chapter

2

At the very bottom of this photograph you can see the rock called the Vishnu Schist, which is some of the oldest rock in the Grand Canyon.

The Making of the Canyon

Scientists believe the earth is about 4.6 billion years old. Rocks from the bottom of the Grand Canyon to its top show nearly 2 billion of these years. The depth of each canyon layer and the kind of rock in it gives scientists clues as to how and when the layer was formed. Further clues come from plant and animal fossils found in certain layers.

Using this information, experts have put together a time line of the area's natural history. The dating is not precise. It is done in millions of years. Furthermore, there are empty spots in the time line. But taken together, the canyon's exposed rocks give scientists an idea of what was happening on that part of the earth during the past 2 billion years.

→ THE BEGINNINGS

The rock at the very bottom of the Grand Canyon is called Vishnu Schist. At about 1.75 million years old, it is some of the oldest rock in the canyon. The oldest dated rock is Elves Chasm gneiss at 1.84 billion years.

Schist is a dark-colored metamorphic rock. Metamorphic rock is made when heat and pressure change rock. In the case of the Vishnu Schist, this happened inside the earth. It was thrust to the earth's surface millions of years ago. No evidence of life has been found in this layer.

THE GREAT UNCONFORMITY

The next rock layer is called the Grand Canyon Supergroup. It was formed 1,250–740 million years ago. This leaves a gap of about 550 million years between the two layers. Why isn't rock there from these years? What was happening on the earth during this time? Canyon rocks yield no clues. This break in geologic history is called an unconformity. In fact, there is an even larger break in areas where the Grand Canyon Supergroup does not exist. In these areas, the Tapeats Sandstone sits directly on the basement rocks. A gap of more than a billion years separates them.

Tapeats Sandstone sits on top of the Grand Canyon Supergroup or, more typically, on the basement rocks. This brown rock was formed about 525 million years ago. This makes another unconformity, or gap in geologic time. This one spans about 190 to 700 million years.

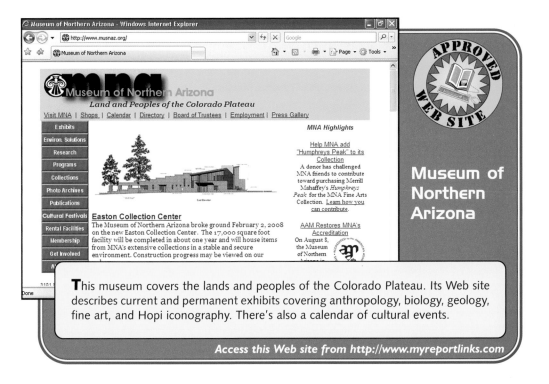

This museum covers the lands and peoples of the Colorado Plateau. Its Web site describes current and permanent exhibits covering anthropology, biology, geology, fine art, and Hopi iconography. There's also a calendar of cultural events.

Access this Web site from http://www.myreportlinks.com

Sandstone is sedimentary rock. It is made when sand or other sediments are pressed into stone. The presence of sandstone indicates that the area was once covered by sea. The water's weight presses the mud and sand below it into rock. The Tapeats layer also contains fossils of trilobites and brachiopods. These primitive water animals provide further evidence that a sea once covered the area.

→THE SEDIMENTS BUILD

Several more sedimentary layers sit on top of the Tapeats Sandstone. First is Bright Angel Shale.

This layer was formed about 515 million years ago. It is a greenish-gray.

Muav Limestone is next. Limestone is made largely from mineral calcite. Much of this calcite comes from the skeletons of marine animals. This also indicates that an ocean once covered the land.

Over the Muav layer is the Temple Butte Formation. Then comes Redwall Limestone. This layer is about 340 million years old. It forms some of the Grand Canyon's steepest cliffs.

Redwall Limestone is naturally gray. However, it has been stained a deep red by iron oxides in the

▲ The rock in the center of this image is Redwall Limestone. The rock was not always red. Over time, iron oxides stained the rock to give it a red appearance.

rock above it. These oxides were leached, or pulled, from the higher layer by water that dripped through it. The oxides were then deposited onto the limestone, turning it red. Or rainfall may have washed the iron oxides onto the rocks below, turning their outer surface red. The Redwall layer is full of caves and arches. It contains fossils of clams, snails, and fish.

By around 300 million years ago, the sea had retreated and the area was a coastal plain. Ferns and conifer trees grew there. Insects buzzed through the air. One giant dragonfly had a wingspan of three feet (ninety-one centimeters). The rocks in this layer are limestone, sandstone, and shale. Together they make the Supai Group.

Above the Supai Group is the Hermit Formation. It is 280 million years old. This layer is a deep red.

⇒ COCONINO

Sometime around 275 million years ago the area became a desert. Sand dunes covered the land. Reptiles, spiders, and insects lived there.

These sand dunes would later be pressed into a light-colored layer called Coconino Sandstone. Coconino lies a few hundred feet below the canyon's rim. Lines run through this layer at steep angles. These show the slopes of the ancient dunes.

The Toroweap Formation is on top of the Coconino Sandstone. It contains both limestone and sandstone. Rocks in this layer range in color from yellow to gray.

About 270 million years ago the land was again covered by a sea. Sponges, sharks, and fish all lived in its waters. The limestone formed during this period is the layer on the canyon's rim. It is called the Kaibab Formation.

The Kaibab Formation is cream to grayish-white. It is the newest rock found in the park. Any rock formed after this period has eroded away.

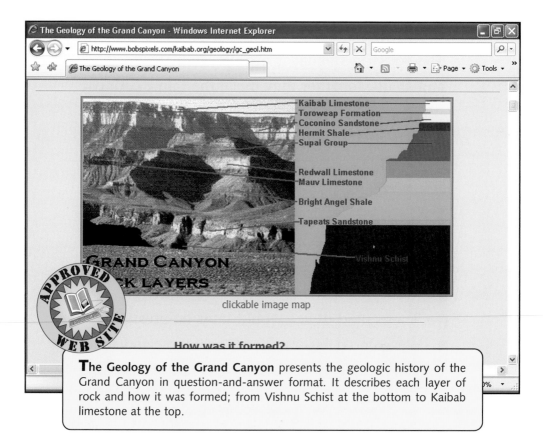

The Geology of the Grand Canyon presents the geologic history of the Grand Canyon in question-and-answer format. It describes each layer of rock and how it was formed; from Vishnu Schist at the bottom to Kaibab limestone at the top.

This final ocean cover lasted until about 60 million years ago. At this time, forces inside the earth pushed the land up, making a huge plateau. The rock that once sat on the sea bottom was now the surface of the land. Layers of older rock lie below it. This land is today's Colorado Plateau.

Then the carving began.

⇒THE RIVER

Six million years ago snowmelt trickled down mountain slopes east of the Colorado Plateau. This trickle joined other trickles to become a stream. Streams flowed together to create a river.

There are a few theories about how the Grand Canyon was formed. The most popular is that the river found its way into Arizona and across the high plateau. Year after year it came, forging a path across the stone. Years turned into decades and decades turned into centuries. Still the river came, eroding limestone and sandstone, then shale and gneiss. They, too, eroded away.

Different kinds of rock reacted differently to the water's eroding power. Some eroded slowly, forming slopes. Others broke off in chunks to make cliffs. Each eroded layer added a new color and shape to the canyon.

Meanwhile, other tributary streams cut into the plateau, making side canyons. Occasionally, their eroding power sliced land from the main plateau to make rock islands. Water and, to a much lesser extent, wind wore some of these buttes into pinnacles.

Today the river has carved its way to a mile below the top of the plateau. Experts think it took from 2 to 5 million years to get there.

Recent geologists feel that a different scenario accounts for the formation of the canyon. It would have been difficult for a river to flow up and over an uplift. They believe that sometime between 5 and 10 million years ago, the Gulf of California opened. Movement along the San Andreas Fault created this opening. This provided a new outlet to the sea. A river began flowing off the southwestern corner of the Colorado Plateau into the Gulf of California. Over time this river carved its way eastward back into the plateau in a process referred to as headward erosion. Eventually, it intercepted and captured the ancestral Colorado River on the eastern side of the Kaibab Uplift.[1]

GEOLOGIC TIME

It is often difficult to comprehend these huge chunks of time. Millions and billions of years are hard to imagine. To help understand this vast time line, one scientist compared the formation of the Grand Canyon to a calendar year.

Using this comparison, the earth would have formed on January 1. Vishnu Schist would have formed on August 14. The canyon's top layer, the Kaibab Formation, would have formed on December 15. And it wasn't until the last day of the year, December 31, that the Colorado River started carving the canyon.[2]

⇒ THE FIRST PEOPLE

The Grand Canyon was already old when the first people wandered into the area about ten thousand years ago.[3] These Paleo-Indians came hunting the bison, mammoths, and mastodons that lived there. The American Indian hunters began settling around the

Scientists differ on what ▷ exactly formed the Grand Canyon. What they do agree on is that millions and billions of years of history are documented in its layers of rocks.

canyon about four thousand years ago. Many probably lived in caves, although this is not certain. Over time they developed a culture, or way of life. They are known as the Desert Culture.

People of the Desert Culture made little figures of sheep and deer from twigs. Dozens of these two- to six-inch (five- to fifteen-centimeter) figurines have been found in caves in the Grand Canyon area. Many have little spears run through them. Experts believe the people used the figures to ask their gods for a successful hunt.[4]

ANCESTRAL PUEBLO

As the centuries passed, the people of the area began growing plants for food. Eventually, they learned to cultivate corn, beans, and squash. Their irrigation systems have been found on the South Rim, on the North Rim, and even on some areas of the Inner Canyon.

Farming made these American Indians less nomadic. They had to stay in one place to tend their crops. Many built mud and stone homes near their fields. Families often lived together in multiroom houses. The foundations of one of their homes can be seen today at Tusayan Pueblo on the South Rim. Another, Walhalla Ruins, has been preserved on the North Rim.

These American Indian farmers are known as Ancestral Pueblo; sometimes they are called the

Anasazi. Ancestral Pueblo lived in the area from about 200 B.C. until around A.D. 1200.

The Ancestral Pueblo wove baskets and sandals from plant leaves. They developed the bow and arrow. They made flutes, pottery, and cloth.

At the same time, another American Indian group related to the Ancestral Pueblo lived to the west. They also built homes along the rim's plateaus. They are known as the Cohonina Indians. Both groups lived next to each other in peace.

Then, around A.D. 1200 to 1300 something caused many of the tribes to leave the area. Some archaeologists think it was a drought. The American Indians moved in small groups to other areas across the Southwest. In time, each group evolved into a specific American Indian tribe. For example, those who moved to mesas east of the Grand Canyon area developed into the Hopi Indians.

Today the Grand Canyon is a sacred place to the Hopi. Some clans believe their people emerged from an earlier world into this world through a hole called a sipapu. This sipapu is in the canyon. Hopi also believe they return to the canyon when they die.[5]

⮕ PAIUTE AND PAI

Around 1300, Paiute Indians moved to the area north of the Grand Canyon from other places in the Southwest. Many of their descendants still live in the region.

Pai Indians came to the South Rim at about the same time. They were the ancestors of the Hualapai and Havasupai Indians. They too live in the area today.

→ CONQUISTADOR

The first Europeans to see the Grand Canyon were Spanish explorers. In 1540 an expedition of three hundred soldiers came to the region looking for gold.

The soldiers were led by conquistador Francisco Vásquez de Coronado. They entered what is now Arizona and then turned east into New

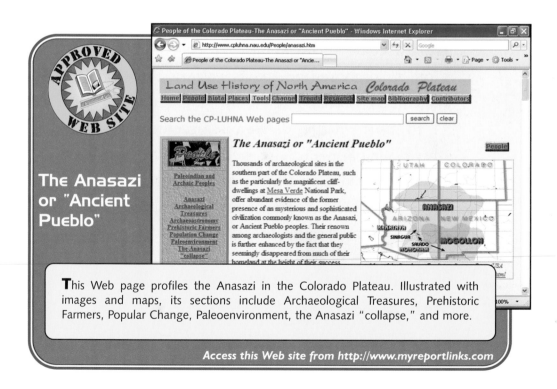

The Anasazi or "Ancient Pueblo"

This Web page profiles the Anasazi in the Colorado Plateau. Illustrated with images and maps, its sections include Archaeological Treasures, Prehistoric Farmers, Popular Change, Paleoenvironment, the Anasazi "collapse," and more.

Access this Web site from http://www.myreportlinks.com

Mexico. From here Coronado sent out a small party to find a river he had heard about from area natives. Coronado wanted to know if it flowed to the Pacific Ocean.

Garcia López de Cárdenas was in charge of the group. Hopi guides took him to the South Rim of the Grand Canyon. They showed him the river below. Some Spaniards tried to climb to the river but could not find a way down.

The Spaniards returned to the main expedition to report that the canyon was impossible to cross. To the Europeans, it was.

None returned to the canyon until 1776. That year Spanish priests came into the region. They wanted to convert the natives there to Christianity. Francisco Tomás Garcés met with the Havasupai down in the canyon. The Havasupai agreed to guide him to the Hopi mesas, and they led him out from the canyon to an area west of today's Grand Canyon Village. There, he first saw the Colorado River. At the time, it was muddy and colored red by sandstone silt. Garcés called it the Rio Colorado—the river colored red.[6]

FIRST AMERICAN SETTLERS

During the first half of the 1800s, American trappers traveled through the area. Most avoided the Grand Canyon.

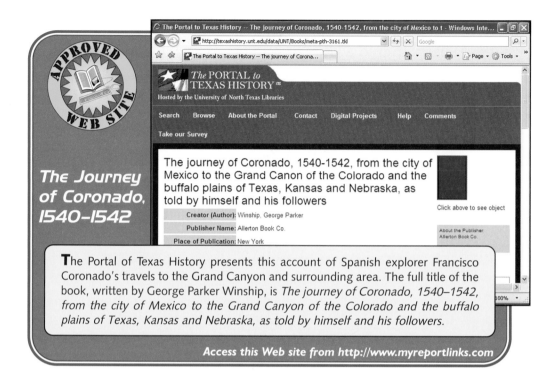

The Journey of Coronado, 1540–1542

The Portal of Texas History presents this account of Spanish explorer Francisco Coronado's travels to the Grand Canyon and surrounding area. The full title of the book, written by George Parker Winship, is *The journey of Coronado, 1540–1542, from the city of Mexico to the Grand Canyon of the Colorado and the buffalo plains of Texas, Kansas and Nebraska, as told by himself and his followers.*

Access this Web site from http://www.myreportlinks.com

At the time, the land was a part of Mexico. In 1848, after the Mexican-American War, the United States and Mexico signed an agreement called the Treaty of Guadalupe Hidalgo. This treaty gave much of what is now the American Southwest to the United States, including the Grand Canyon.

Even before the treaty, though, Americans had been settling on land around the canyon. Mormons had migrated to present-day Utah in 1847. As their numbers grew, they looked for more places to live. By 1850, Mormon scouts had reached the North Rim of the Grand Canyon.

The U.S. Army began exploring the area in 1857. That year Lieutenant Joseph Ives led an expedition into the region. The Ives Expedition started at the Gulf of California, where the Colorado River flowed into the ocean. Ives took a steamboat up the river. He got about as far as where Arizona, Nevada, and California now meet. At that point, the river became too rough to navigate, so the group left the boat. They mounted mules they had brought and went off to explore the river's western canyons, going as far upstream as Diamond Creek near Peach Springs, Arizona. This expedition produced the first map of the area.

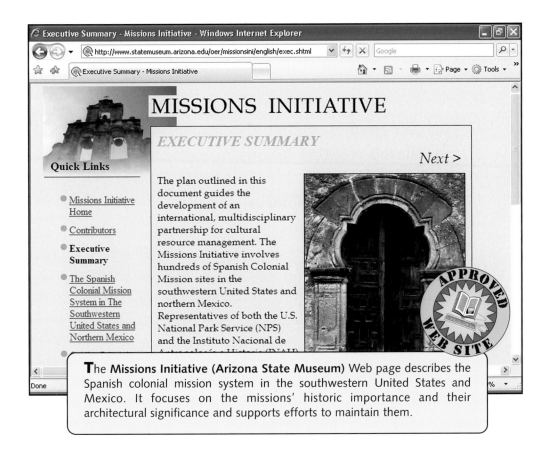

The **Missions Initiative (Arizona State Museum)** Web page describes the Spanish colonial mission system in the southwestern United States and Mexico. It focuses on the missions' historic importance and their architectural significance and supports efforts to maintain them.

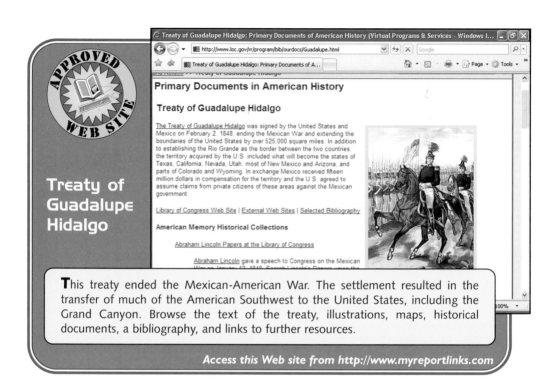

Primary Documents in American History

Treaty of Guadalupe Hidalgo

The Treaty of Guadalupe Hidalgo was signed by the United States and Mexico on February 2, 1848, ending the Mexican War and extending the boundaries of the United States by over 525,000 square miles. In addition to establishing the Rio Grande as the border between the two countries, the territory acquired by the U.S. included what will become the states of Texas, California, Nevada, Utah, most of New Mexico and Arizona, and parts of Colorado and Wyoming. In exchange Mexico received fifteen million dollars in compensation for the territory and the U.S. agreed to assume claims from private citizens of these areas against the Mexican government.

Library of Congress Web Site | External Web Sites | Selected Bibliography

American Memory Historical Collections

Abraham Lincoln Papers at the Library of Congress

Abraham Lincoln gave a speech to Congress on the Mexican

Treaty of Guadalupe Hidalgo

This treaty ended the Mexican-American War. The settlement resulted in the transfer of much of the American Southwest to the United States, including the Grand Canyon. Browse the text of the treaty, illustrations, maps, historical documents, a bibliography, and links to further resources.

Access this Web site from http://www.myreportlinks.com

Ives called the region valueless. He predicted that his group would be "the last party of whites to visit this profitless locality."[7]

⇒ JOHN WESLEY POWELL

Ives was wrong. In just eleven years, John Wesley Powell was exploring the region. Powell was a Civil War veteran who had lost an arm in battle. Retired from the Army and intrigued by the West, Powell organized a trip to the Grand Canyon.

In 1869, he and nine other men started off at Green River, Wyoming. They followed the Green to the Colorado, then paddled into the unknown. Just a month into their journey the group encountered rapids that destroyed one of their boats. Afterward, one man told Powell, "I've had more excitement than a man deserves in a lifetime. I'm leaving."[8] This all occurred while Powell was still on the Green River.

Powell and the others continued downriver. During the next two months, the explorers came across more rapids. After a particularly perilous one, some of the men begged Powell to abandon his quest. He refused. The next day three more men left the group. They walked out through a

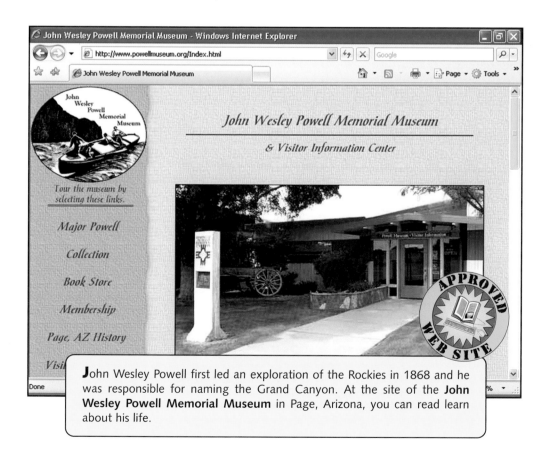

John Wesley Powell first led an exploration of the Rockies in 1868 and he was responsible for naming the Grand Canyon. At the site of the **John Wesley Powell Memorial Museum** in Page, Arizona, you can read learn about his life.

side canyon but were soon killed by either American Indians or Mormon settlers.

Two days later, Powell and the remaining men reached the mouth of the Virgin River. Mormon settlers greeted them there.

All along the journey, Powell had kept notes about the plants, animals, and rocks of the region. Powell's journal also showed an appreciation for the area's beauty. In one entry, Powell wrote, "The glories and the beauties of form, color and sound unite in the Grand Canyon. . . ."[9]

Powell and others had described the canyon as grand, and the name stuck. Ever since his journey, the great chasm has been known as the Grand Canyon.[10]

From 1871 until 1874, Powell took other trips through the Grand Canyon. This expedition produced a map, photographs, and more observations.

In 1873, artist Thomas Moran joined the expedition. Moran's sketches would later be included in Powell's publications. Moran would also paint *The Chasm of the Colorado* as a result of his trip. The U.S. Congress bought the painting and hung it in the U.S. Capitol Building.

⇒MINERS AND HORSE THIEVES

Before long, miners were headed to the region. They braved the desolate and dangerous terrain with burros loaded with supplies. Some found copper and asbestos. Few found anything. So most miners abandoned their claims and left the region. They also left their burros, whose descendants still roam the area.

By the late 1800s, horse thieves had also discovered the Grand Canyon. Many stole horses in Utah and drove them into the canyon on a North Rim trail. While in the canyon, they changed the brands on the horses so they could not be identified. Then the thieves drove the horses farther into Arizona Territory and sold them. Enough stolen horses were herded through the canyon that one trail became known as Horsethief Trail.

Thomas Moran was a famous painter of his era who accompanied John Wesley Powell's expedition to the Grand Canyon.

⊜AMERICAN INDIAN RESERVATIONS

Around that time, American settlers were also moving into the area. Some pushed American Indians off their land. This led to battles between them. One series of battles was known as the Hualapai Wars.

In an effort to open land for the Americans, the U.S. government forced Hualapai Indians from their homes after the Hualapai Wars. Soldiers marched them across Arizona and made them live

The Havasupai American Indian nation lost most of its land when Grand Canyon National Park was designated. They regained much of it in 1975. The **Havasupai Indian Reservation** Web site describes its history and current operations and offers maps for those who want to camp, hike, or otherwise visit the area.

in a special camp. Many Hualapai died at the camp from disease and lack of food.[11]

A year later the Hualapai were told they could return to their homelands, under one condition—they had to live on land the settlers did not want. This portion of the Hualapai's original lands, a million acres, became the Hualapai Indian Reservation.

As for the Havasupai, they were also restricted to a reservation. The Havasupai Reservation was in a corner of a side canyon. It, too, was only a small part of the land the Havasupai once occupied.

➔ TOURISM COMES TO THE CANYON

By the late 1880s some miners had found a new way to make money. They began lodging tourists visiting the area. One miner, John Hance, lodged so many guests in tents surrounding his log cabin that it became known as the Hance Hotel.

Hance entertained his visitors with tall tales. He often told them that he had built the Grand Canyon. "It was hard work," he would say. "Took a long time, but I dug it myself, with a pick and a shovel."[12] Not surprisingly, Hance became known as the Grand Canyon's biggest liar.

In 1897 a miner named Pete Berry was considering abandoning his claim, the Last Chance Mine. He built the Grand View Hotel at Grandview Point near Hance's cabin. Berry took many of his guests into the canyon on burros he had once used for mining. Most of these tourists came to the Grand-view area from Flagstaff. They traveled by wagon on a rough dirt road. Berry sold the claim to his mine in 1901 to focus on tourism.

THE RAILROAD

Sightseers were also traveling to the area west of Grandview Point. Guests there stayed at the Bright Angel Hotel. Built in 1896, it was the first hotel in what would become Grand Canyon Village.

In 1901 the Santa Fe Railroad opened a railroad line from Williams to the Grand Canyon. The line ended near the Bright Angel Hotel. Now tourists could ride to the canyon in the relative comfort of a train.

In 1905 the railroad built its own hotel near the Bright Angel. El Tovar Hotel was large and luxurious. It looked like a cross between a Swiss chalet and a hunting lodge.

THE KOLB BROTHERS

Other businesses were moving into the area, too. Brothers Emery and Ellsworth Kolb had come to the canyon in the early 1900s. They set up a dark-room in a tent.

The Kolbs took souvenir photographs for visitors. They also explored the area, taking some of the first pictures of the park's backcountry. By 1904 the brothers had built themselves a real studio in the growing village.

From 1911 to 1912 the Kolbs retraced Powell's trip down the Colorado River. They filmed their journey. It was the first motion picture of the canyon by river. The Kolbs then traveled around the country showing the film and telling about their adventure.

Before long, Grand Canyon Village was the center of tourist activity. Most visitors preferred the comfortable train ride there over the wagon

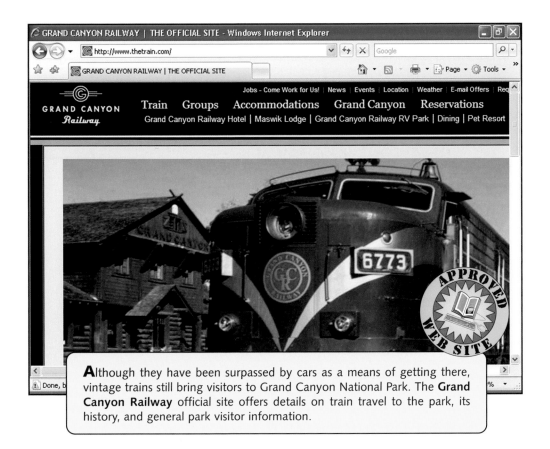

Although they have been surpassed by cars as a means of getting there, vintage trains still bring visitors to Grand Canyon National Park. The **Grand Canyon Railway** official site offers details on train travel to the park, its history, and general park visitor information.

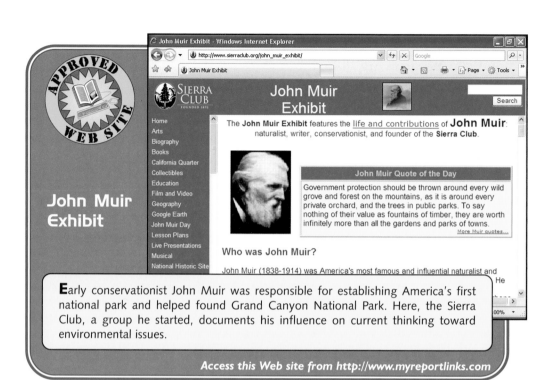

Access this Web site from http://www.myreportlinks.com

ride to Grandview Point. In time, the Grand View Hotel closed due to lack of business.

⟶ PROTECTING THE LAND

Between the railroad, the Kolb brothers, and Thomas Moran's art, the Grand Canyon was getting a lot of advertising. The publicity was well received. Many Americans were anxious to visit the area. Furthermore, they were interested in keeping it as natural as possible.

Back in 1893, President Benjamin Harrison had made the Grand Canyon a National Forest Preserve. This title gave the area some protection from development. However, it still allowed people to mine and log the land.

President Theodore Roosevelt had visited the canyon in the early 1900s. He called it "the one great sight every American should see."[13] In 1906, he made parts of the region into a National Game Preserve. Hunting on the preserve was prohibited.

In 1908 the two preserves were combined. They were then given a new designation: the Grand Canyon National Monument. This status meant that no one could build a house or business there without permission from the federal government.

A NATIONAL PARK

By 1910 many people recognized the unique value and beauty of the Grand Canyon. They wanted the area protected from all development. They also wanted it to be open to the American public. Short and simple, they wanted it made into a national park. The United States already had several national parks. These areas were protected and preserved for the enjoyment of all U.S. citizens.

By 1919, Congress had passed a bill that would make the area a national park. It was then sent on to President Woodrow Wilson for approval. President Wilson signed the bill on February 26, 1919, and the Grand Canyon became the country's seventeenth national park.

Chapter

3

Due to its remote location, one of the first challenges facing the creators of Grand Canyon National Park was building roads through the untouched desert.

The New Park

Creating Grand Canyon National Park (GCNP) was just a start. Now the area had to be made accessible for the ordinary sightseer.

→ ROADS

One of the first tasks was improving roads. The new park had no paved roads. Motorists who braved its dirt roads carried their own tools in case of breakdowns. Bus drivers traveled with carrier pigeons. When their bus got stuck, they released one. It would fly to a nearby service station to signal that help was needed.[1]

The first road to receive attention was the road that traveled east from Grand Canyon Village. Workers widened and leveled the road, using nothing but hand tools. On the North Rim, the main road to Point Imperial was also improved. But this only meant making a dirt road out of a trail of ruts.

Yet these basic improvements were not enough. The number of people coming to GCNP by car was increasing. Soon it would exceed the amount coming by train. By summer 1925 it was clear that GCNP roads needed to be paved.

The paving was carefully planned. All roads were designed to follow the flattest route possible that would give visitors the most scenic views. They would also have several pullouts for canyon overlooks. The paving began in the late 1920s. It took several years to finish the work.

⇒PARK LODGING

The new national park already had hotels, but park officials wanted lodging for those who could not afford to stay in them. In 1920, GCNP opened its first campground. In 1922 a second campground opened. Both of these were free to visitors on a first-come, first-served basis.

Park officials also wanted to provide housing at the bottom of the canyon. In 1922, cabins and a main lodge building were erected there on the north side of the river. The site was named Phantom Ranch, after nearby Phantom Creek.

Phantom Ranch was made with as many nearby materials as possible. This saved having to bring supplies down the canyon by mule. Hence the lodge was made mostly of rocks. During the

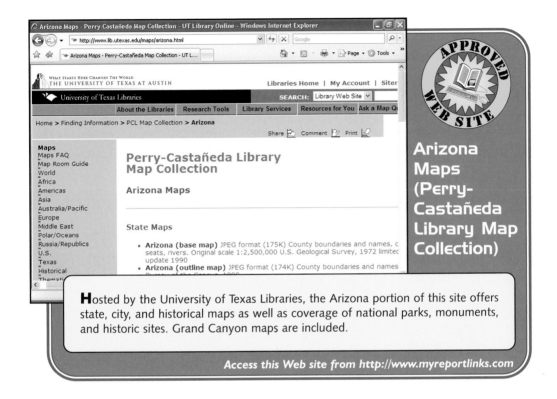

Hosted by the University of Texas Libraries, the Arizona portion of this site offers state, city, and historical maps as well as coverage of national parks, monuments, and historic sites. Grand Canyon maps are included.

Access this Web site from http://www.myreportlinks.com

next decade, eight cabins were built near Phantom Ranch for more lodging.

WATER

The new park's most challenging problem was water. The dry areas on the rims had few natural water sources. At first, trains brought water from Del Rio, Arizona, to GCNP. Tankers hauled 100,000 gallons (378,541 liters) of water a day to the park. But this was expensive. For many years scientists looked for springs that could provide plentiful water. It wasn't until 1932 that a dependable source was developed for the South Rim.

⇒ TRAILS

Another priority in the early 1920s was trail improvement. Many of the park's existing trails were old mining trails or American Indian routes. Most were overgrown and eroded, so men were hired to clear the old trails. They worked with nothing more than shovels and sticks.

Park officials also wanted to connect a trail from one rim to the other. This required a bridge. In 1921 a wooden suspension bridge was built over the river. But this bridge was flimsy and unstable.

In 1928 a steel bridge was built to replace it. Kaibab Suspension Bridge was 440 feet (134 meters) long and five feet (two meters) wide. It is still in use today.

⇒ THE MYSTERY OF GLEN AND BESSIE HYDE

As the bridge was being built, newlyweds Glen and Bessie Hyde were planning an adventurous honeymoon. They wanted to boat down the Colorado River through the Grand Canyon. Bessie would be the first woman to do so.

The couple launched from Green River, Utah, in October 1928, without life jackets. Twenty-six days later they reached the bottom of the Bright Angel Trail. The two climbed to the South Rim and posed for a picture at Kolb Studio.

Some reports say that Bessie wanted to quit at this point. Glen, however, insisted they continue. They headed back into the Canyon.

A month later, the Hydes' boat was found floating peacefully in the middle of the river. All of their belongings were in it. But the Hydes were gone. Neither was ever seen again.

A search yielded no trace of either one. They seemed to have vanished. Since their disappearance, theories and legends have arisen regarding the Hydes. Some people think they drowned. Others think one may have killed the other and left

▲ Glen and Bessie Hyde posed for a picture at the bottom of Bright Angel Trail, part of which is shown here. It was the last picture of them alive.

the canyon in secret to start a new life. To this day, the mystery has not been solved.[2]

⊖CIVILIAN CONSERVATION CORPS

In 1933, Civilian Conservation Corps (CCC) workers came to the park. This federal program employed men who were out of work during the Great Depression.

CCC workers made many improvements. They improved roads and constructed buildings. They built trails. They built a mule corral and ranger station near Phantom Ranch. They even built a

Hoover Dam, located near Las Vegas, Nevada, was the largest dam in the world when it was completed in 1936. The creation of the dam slowed the flow of the Colorado River through the Grand Canyon.

three-room schoolhouse for the children who lived in Grand Canyon Village.

As the Great Depression ended, the CCC was disbanded. Workers left GCNP in 1942 having made several upgrades to the park.

HOOVER DAM

The 1930s brought another project to the area. Engineers had designed a huge dam that would span a canyon just west of the park. Black Canyon was on the Nevada-Arizona border. A dam across it would stop seasonal flooding in the valleys downriver from the Grand Canyon. It would also store water and make electricity for growing desert towns such as Las Vegas, Nevada.

Workers started building the Hoover Dam in March 1931. When it was completed in 1936, it was the world's largest dam. At its base it was as thick as two football fields.

Soon the Hoover Dam began backing up the waters of the Colorado River. This created Lake Mead near Las Vegas, Nevada. This reservoir covers almost 250 square miles (647 square kilometers) of land.

GLEN CANYON DAM

During the 1940s some people wanted to build a second dam along the Colorado River. This one would be northeast of the Grand Canyon near present-day

51

Page, Arizona. It too would store water and generate electricity for a growing population. This dam would back up water into Glen Canyon.

Many people opposed the dam. They knew that flooding Glen Canyon would mean a loss of scenery and ecosystems there. They were also concerned about ecosystems in the Grand Canyon. Many groups tried to stop the dam from being built. They lost.

The building began in 1956 and was finished in 1963. The resulting reservoir was named Lake Powell. It too was huge.

⊜A New River

The Glen Canyon Dam had an effect on the plants and animals of GCNP. The new dam regulated the flow of water through the canyon. This meant the Colorado River no longer surged and receded with the seasons, rain, or snowmelt. This caused a lot of changes.

First was a reduction in the river's beaches. Flooding had always brought new sand and sediment onto the beaches inside the Grand Canyon. This sediment replaced what was washed downriver. However, without flooding there was no new replacement sand. Soon the river's beaches grew smaller. Some even disappeared.

Without the sediments brought by rushing water, the water became clearer. This allowed

Living Rivers Home Page - Windows Internet Explorer

http://www.livingrivers.org/index.cfm

Google

Living Rivers Home Page

Page ▾ Tools ▾

LIVING RIVERS
COLORADO RIVERKEEPER®

Search

Home | About | News | Campaigns | Join

Headlines

September 11, 2008
LR Letter
Proposed pump station, reservoirs and hydroelectric powerplant in Grand County, Utah.

September 9, 2008
Regional News
Crucial Grand Canyon sandbars have rapidly eroded

August 27, 2008
Regional News
Poll says half of Nevadans willing to live with tighter restrictions on water use

August 25, 2008
Regional News
McCain stirs uproar with call for

save grand canyon
from glen canyon dam

the end of lake powe
It's not a matter of if, but

"No man ever steps in the same river twice, for it's not the same river and he's n - Heraclitas

About Living Rivers

Join our Email list

Living Rivers seeks to involve the public in efforts to restore rivers to their natural status. At **Living Rivers: Colorado Riverkeeper** you can learn about the group's opposition to Glen Canyon Dam and efforts to have it removed.

more sunlight into the water. Now algae and other plants grew in the river. This gave the water a green color. Before long, the Colorado River was no longer a red-tinged river colored by sand and silt. The river was now clear and green.

The new algae became food for insects and fish. These in turn became food for birds, lizards, and other animals. With this steady source of food, the number of animals along the river increased.

The dam helped animals in another way. Before it was built, flooding often washed away beachside plants. But without the flooding, many plants had a chance to grow and flourish. This created more homes for animals.

Yet the dam had a negative effect on some species. The new Colorado River was colder than the old one. The old river had been full of fish that liked warm water and had learned to survive the water's seasonal changes. These same fish, however, could not adjust to the colder water. Many died.

This was made worse when the river was stocked with a nonnative fish: trout. Native species could not compete with the trout. More of the river's original fish species died. In time, some

▲ Some environmentalists charge that the Glen Canyon Dam, shown here, has hurt the wildlife in both Lake Powell and the Colorado River.

species even disappeared. Today only two native fish species are very common in the canyon.[3] They are the bluehead sucker and the speckled dace.

Increased numbers of trout led to other changes in the ecosystem. Trout are a favored food of the bald eagle. There were few bald eagles in the canyon before the dam. But now the Colorado held an abundant food source for them, and the number of eagles along the river increased.

⮕ BOUNDARY CHANGES AND WORLDWIDE RECOGNITION

In 1975 the Grand Canyon National Park Enlargement Act was enacted, declaring that the U.S. government had to give back land it had taken from the Havasupai Indians in the 1880s. Suddenly, the Havasupai Reservation grew from 518 acres to 185,000 acres.[4]

That same year, the park gained land. Congress added nearby federal lands to GCNP. With the new land, the size of the park nearly doubled.

In 1979 the Grand Canyon was given global recognition when it was named a World Heritage Site. This meant it was considered by scientists all over the world to be important to the planet.

⮕ PROTECTING THE CONDOR AND OTHER SPECIES

During the 1970s and 1980s, the American public had become increasingly aware of environmental

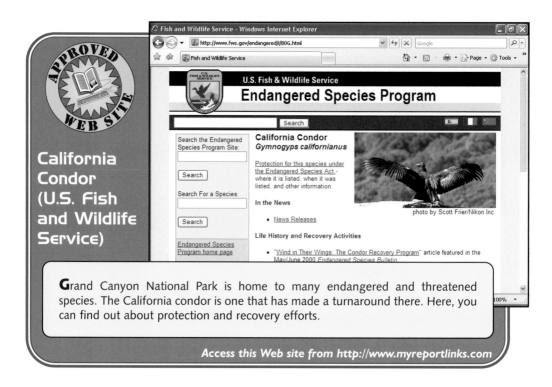

California
Condor
(U.S. Fish
and Wildlife
Service)

Grand Canyon National Park is home to many endangered and threatened species. The California condor is one that has made a turnaround there. Here, you can find out about protection and recovery efforts.

Access this Web site from http://www.myreportlinks.com

issues. With this awareness came concern about protecting the country's endangered and threatened animal species.

One species, the California condor, was in danger of becoming extinct. This bird had once lived around the Grand Canyon. But its numbers were decreasing everywhere. Habitat destruction, poaching, and lead poisoning shared the blame. By 1982 only twenty-two condors remained in the wild.[5]

Soon several groups were working to capture and raise these birds in captivity. Once there were enough condors, the Peregrine Fund planned to release them back into the wild.

By 1996 the group was ready to release some condors into the area. Many were released in Arizona. Some of these nested in GCNP. Today there is a healthy population of condors inside the park. Private groups are still monitoring them. They hope to keep the birds healthy and safe for years to come.

In addition to the condors, GCNP provides a safe home to ten other endangered or threatened animals. These include the desert gopher tortoise, the Southwestern willow flycatcher, and the Mexican spotted owl.

GCNP is also a refuge for species and sub-species that live nowhere else in the world. The white-tailed Kaibab squirrel and the Grand Canyon pink rattlesnake are two of the most common.

An endangered species, the California condor is making a slow recovery. This condor has been tagged for tracking, allowing scientists to monitor its life cycle and help the species.

Grand Canyon National Park: Oh Ranger! is a park overview with guides to park activities, history, flora and fauna, and much more. The site also spotlights people involved in making and supporting the park.

EDITOR'S CHOICE

⊖ TOMORROW'S PARK

Water is still shaping GCNP. The park's hard desert soil cannot absorb much water. So when it rains, water rushes across the land and spills down canyon walls. It often takes rocks, soil, and plants with it. Rains and freezing water also continue to erode the park's stone towers.

The Colorado River is changing the canyon, too. The rock on today's riverbed is mainly granite in most areas. Granite is harder than sedimentary rock, and it will take longer for the water to erode it. Even so, the river carves a tiny bit deeper into canyon rocks every year.

⊜THE SOUTH RIM

Most visitors come to GCNP from the south. Many arrive at the park's east entrance from Flagstaff, Arizona.

Just inside the entrance is the Desert View developed area. This is the highest point of the South Rim. It is nearly 7,500 feet (2,286 meters) above sea level. National Park Service (NPS) rangers and Grand Canyon Association employees provide canyon information. The Desert View Bookstore/Park Information Center also houses a small bookstore.

Desert View Watchtower sits nearby on the edge of the South Rim. The Watchtower was built in 1933.

Grandview Point was once one of the busiest places in Grand Canyon National Park. It is still a popular landmark for snapping photos.

The façade of the seventy-foot (twenty-one-meter) lookout is made from area stone. Inside, tourists can admire murals painted by Hopi artist Fred Kabotie. At the top is a spectacular view of the Painted Desert and Marble Canyon.

⇒ LANDMARKS IN THE SOUTH RIM

From there Desert View Drive skirts the south side of the canyon for twenty-six miles (forty-two kilometers). Along the length of the road are many canyon overlooks. There are also several places of educational and historical interest.

One of the first overlooks is Lipan Point. The view is of the Colorado River and Unkar Delta. Ancestral Pueblo lived and farmed on this sandy soil just north of the river.

Farther west is Tusayan Ruin and Museum. Tusayan is the word the Spanish used for Hopi territory. Here visitors can walk among the remains of an eight-hundred-year-old American Indian village. It is believed that about thirty Ancestral Pueblo once lived in this fourteen-room structure.

A self-guided tour moves visitors past the stone foundations of their kivas, living areas, and storage rooms. The Tusayan Museum has a display of twig figures created by the earlier Desert Culture people, as well as other displays featuring native cultures both historic and modern.

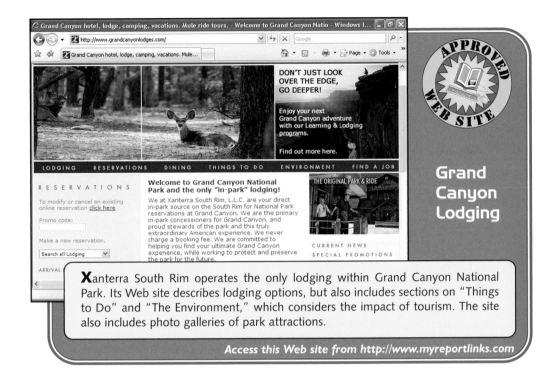

Xanterra South Rim operates the only lodging within Grand Canyon National Park. Its Web site describes lodging options, but also includes sections on "Things to Do" and "The Environment," which considers the impact of tourism. The site also includes photo galleries of park attractions.

Access this Web site from http://www.myreportlinks.com

The next stop is Moran Point, named for Thomas Moran. The overlook offers a view of the butte called Vishnu Temple. Vishnu Temple looks something like a birthday cake with one fat candle.

Grandview Point, where John Hance once resided, is next. During the 1890s this was one of the busiest places in the canyon.

Pipe Creek Vista is several miles down the road. This is the trailhead for the Rim Trail. This path travels west along the canyon rim. It is paved and nearly flat. There are plans to extend the Rim Trail.

Just beyond Pipe Creek, Highway 64 turns south and heads out of the park toward Williams. If you were to turn north instead, you would continue along the rim on South Entrance Road. This is the road that feeds into Village Loop in the village area.

The next stop on South Entrance Road is Mather Point. The lookout here boasts a 180-degree view of the canyon. The Colorado River can be seen below.

INFO AND HOTELS

Canyon View Information Plaza is a short walk from Mather Point's parking lot. Outdoor kiosks tell visitors about trails, tours, and activities. Canyon View Information Plaza houses several displays and a bookstore. Rangers on duty answer questions and give present informational programs.

On down the road is Park Headquarters, the business offices of the park. To the north are Mather Amphitheater and a trail that leads to the Rim Trail. To the south are campgrounds, a grocery store, Yavapai Lodge, and restrooms.

Farther west are several hotels and the original Grand Canyon Depot. During the canyon's early days a railroad agent lived in the second story of this old log building. Today the second floor houses park offices. The first floor operates a ticket booth for the trains that still bring tourists to the canyon.

Just across the road, El Tovar Hotel hugs the canyon rim. The building is now a National Historic Landmark. In addition to lodging, it has a dining room, a lounge, and a couple of small shops. Two porch swings on El Tovar's back deck provide comfortable seating for canyon viewing.

Close by is Hopi House, which opened in 1905. It houses a collection of American Indian arts and crafts. Another building farther west along the rim, Lookout Studio, holds a gift shop along with a viewing platform.

A short walk on the Rim Trail leads to Kolb Studio. This is the photography studio that the Kolb brothers built in 1904. The building now houses a

▲ *Grand Canyon Lodge is a place to stay for visitors of Grand Canyon National Park. It also provides one of the best views of the canyon below.*

bookstore and an art gallery with changing displays inspired by the canyon. Some of the Kolbs' belongings are also on display.

Grand Canyon Village is also home to horse and mule stables. Many of these animals are regulars on the Bright Angel Trail that starts nearby. This trail goes to Phantom Ranch at the bottom of the canyon.

Hermit Road travels seven miles (11.3 kilometers) farther west. From March through November the road is open only to the free park shuttle buses. The pavement on the Rim Trail ends at Maricopa Point. The path, however, continues to the end of the road.

Just down Hermit Road is the Powell Memorial, where a monument honors explorer John Wesley Powell. The last viewpoint on this road is Hermits Rest. It was named for "Hermit" Louis Boucher, who lived in the canyon below Hermits Rest for twenty-one years. Hermits Rest is one of the park's best sunset-watching points.

THE NORTH RIM

Only 10 percent of the people who come to GCNP visit the North Rim.[6] Those who do arrive on Arizona Highway 67 from Jacob Lake. Snow closes this road every fall and winter. Therefore, most North Rim services and facilities are only open from mid-May to mid-October.

The main road into the park forks about twelve miles (19.3 kilometers) from the entrance. One fork continues south toward the North Rim Campground. A few of its campsites sit on the canyon's rim. The North Kaibab Trail starts nearby. It is the North Rim developed area's only trail to the bottom.

Close by is the North Rim Visitor Center. It holds exhibits and a bookstore. Rangers here answer questions and lead interpretive programs.

The road ends at Grand Canyon Lodge. This stone building boasts a fifty-foot (15.2-meter) ceiling with three enormous windows. Each one

▲ This view is from Walhalla Overlook, one of the more popular scenic overlooks in Grand Canyon National Park.

Descending the Grand Canyon by mule has always been a popular way to make it down the chasm.

offers a spectacular view of the canyon. Log cabins for canyon visitors surround the lodge. There are also other rooms that look more like standard motel rooms.

A trail from the lodge leads to Bright Angel Point. This point has a stunning view of Bright Angel Canyon.

Back at the fork, the main road travels east toward the Walhalla Plateau. A short road from here leads to Point Imperial. At 8,803 feet (2,683 meters), this is the highest viewpoint on the North Rim. It overlooks the Painted Desert and the eastern end of the Grand Canyon.

The road continues south along the top of the Walhalla Plateau. Scenic lookouts line the route. At Walhalla Overlook, a dirt path takes visitors to Walhalla Ruins. Here the foundations from Ancestral Pueblo homes can be seen.

⇨ PATHS IN THE PARK

At the end of the road is a paved path. It leads to a rock peninsula that sticks out over the Grand Canyon. All around it are sheer drops and stunning views. Underneath is Angels Window, a natural arch caused by wind and flash flood erosion. Back on the original path, the trail continues to the tip of Cape Royal. Vishnu Temple sits across the void.

There is another road that travels along the North Rim from the Visitor Center. This rugged dirt road requires a four-wheel drive vehicle. It is so rough that it takes two hours to travel its seventeen-mile (27.4-kilometer) length to Point Sublime.

The portion of the park west of there can only by reached by an unpaved road from Arizona Highway 389 near Fredonia, Arizona. This road leads to Toroweap Overlook. It is also known as Tuweep. Toroweap Overlook is about three thousand feet (914 meters) above the Colorado River. The river is nearly straight down.

Nearby is a cave filled with stunning prehistoric paintings. These red, white, green, and orange images include forty humanlike figures. Some have flattened heads, some are stick figures, and some are bent bodies with outstretched hands. Images of birds sixty feet (18.3 meters) wide have also been painted here.[7]

These pictures are thought to be two to four thousand years old. Experts think they were part of some ancient canyon dwellers' religious ceremonies. For this reason, the cave is called Shaman's Gallery. A shaman is a religious leader. The exact location of Shaman's Gallery is kept a secret to protect it from vandals.

THE INNER CANYON

Thousands of people travel to the bottom of the Grand Canyon every year. All come by foot, horse, mule, river, or even helicopter.

One of the most traveled trails from the South Rim is the old American Indian path, Bright Angel Trail. Another trail is the South Kaibab Trail. Visitors can get to the bottom from the North Rim, too. Most descend on the North Kaibab Trail.

The Kaibab Suspension Bridge still stands at the bottom of the canyon. A second bridge, Bright Angel Suspension Bridge, offers another option for crossing the river. It was built in the 1960s.

All of these trails meet up at Phantom Ranch. In addition to the lodge and its cabins, the Phantom Ranch area includes dormitories, an amphitheater, campfire circle, campgrounds for backpackers, and mule stables.

Whether viewed from the North Rim, South Rim, or Inner Canyon, the geology of the Grand Canyon is awesome. Its rock features, striking colors, and huge voids are an almost otherworldly experience. GCNP is more than rocks, though. It is home to many interesting plants and animals.

Chapter 4

The Gila monster is one of the largest lizards found in Grand Canyon National Park. Be careful, it's poisonous.

Plant and Animal Life

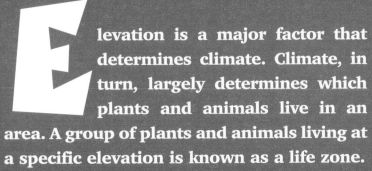

Elevation is a major factor that determines climate. Climate, in turn, largely determines which plants and animals live in an area. A group of plants and animals living at a specific elevation is known as a life zone.

Elevations inside GCNP differ by as much as 8,000 feet (2,438 meters). This vast difference creates five distinct life zones in the park. Each one contains special plants and animals.

Of course, life zones do not have walls around them. Many plants and animals cross the zones. Furthermore, wind, moisture, and sun exposure can all create microclimates within a zone. These host their own mini-ecosystems. In general, though, GCNP can be divided into the Riparian, Lower Sonoran, Upper Sonoran, Transition, and Boreal life zones.

→ RIPARIAN

A riparian ecosystem is based on water. The Colorado River and the streams that flow into it create GCNP's riparian environments.

Algae and crustaceans are abundant in the river. Both are an important source of food for its fish. Twenty-five fish species live in park waters. Carp and rainbow trout are two of the most common. Both are nonnative species that had been introduced to the park by humans.

Two plants dominate Colorado River beaches: the coyote willow and tamarisk. Tamarisk is a dense-growing shrub or tree. It has bluish-green leaves. Young plants have skinny, flexible stalks.

Coyote willow grows about fifteen feet (five meters) tall. Its long, narrow leaves grow on slender green stems. This willow flowering plant likes to be near water and does well in sandy soil.

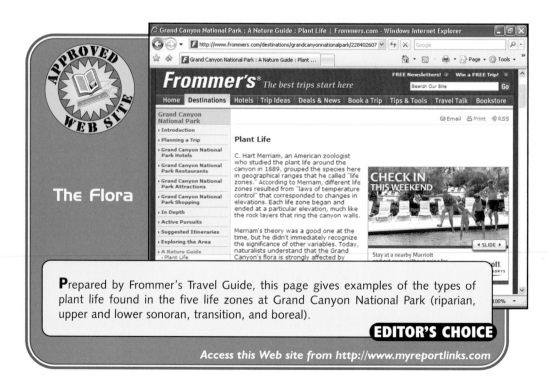

Prepared by Frommer's Travel Guide, this page gives examples of the types of plant life found in the five life zones at Grand Canyon National Park (riparian, upper and lower sonoran, transition, and boreal).

Access this Web site from http://www.myreportlinks.com

➲PARK ANIMALS

Many animals live amongst the tamarisk and willow thickets. The canyon tree frog and the red-spotted toad are common. So are lizards. The Gila monster and the chuckwalla are two of the largest lizards in the canyon. The Gila monster can grow to two feet (sixty-one centimeters) in length.

Chuckwallas grow to eighteen inches (forty-six centimeters) long. They are brown with a dark head. Loose skin hangs from their body. When predators threaten, chuckwallas move into rocks and inflate their skin. This wedges them in place so they can't be pried loose.

Many different pests live near the water. These include mayflies, black flies, mites, beetles, butterflies, and fire ants.

Numerous spiders also inhabit this zone. Scorpions live here, too. The largest scorpions are about four inches (ten centimeters) long. They are tan-colored bugs with two pincers. Their long tail curls toward their head.

Antelope squirrels and pocket mice also live among the thickets. They are often prey to the ringtails that reside here. Ringtails are relatives of the raccoon. They are gray with a white-banded tail. Ringtails are so smart they can untie knots.

Snakes also dine on the area's insects and small rodents. GCNP is home to six kinds of rattlesnakes. The Grand Canyon pink rattlesnake is the most common. It is found only in the Grand Canyon. This snake is often seen near water. It has pinkish skin with dark blotches that help it blend in with the canyon soil.

COTTONWOODS

Fremont cottonwood trees dot the streams that flow into the Colorado River. These large trees are covered with grooved bark. They can grow to more than sixty feet (eighteen meters) tall and three feet (ninety-one centimeters) thick.

Many birds depend on these riverside trees. In fact, of the 355 different species of birds that live in GCNP, 250 of them are found near the river. However, only forty-eight of these live along the river all year long. The rest migrate in winter.

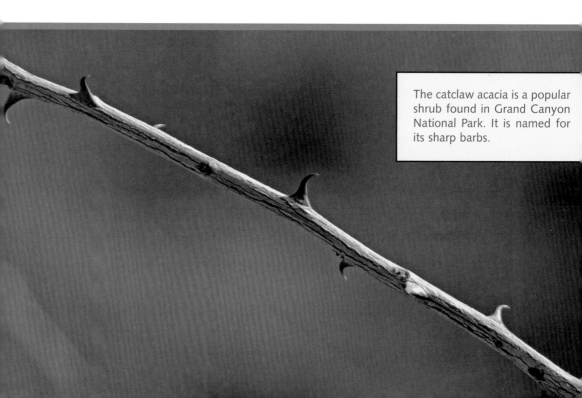

The catclaw acacia is a popular shrub found in Grand Canyon National Park. It is named for its sharp barbs.

Ducks, for example, are more abundant along the river in the winter.

Bald eagles also spend the winter here. The trout-rich waters provide them with plenty of food. These eagles have a brown body with a white head and neck. Their wingspan can stretch beyond seven feet (two meters).

⇒ UPPER AND LOWER SONORAN

Just above the river is a hot, dry region where plants compete for water. The Lower Sonoran life zone lies at elevations from 100 to 4,000 feet (30 to 1,200 meters). Above it is the Upper Sonoran life zone. It stretches from 4,000 to 7,000 feet (1,200 to 2,100 meters). The soil here is thin and rock is just a few inches below the surface.

Both the western honey mesquite tree and the catclaw acacia tree grow along canyon walls just above the river and creeks. Both trees can grow to twenty feet (six meters). The mesquite grows seedpods that are several inches long. Mesquite seeds, or beans, were eaten by Ancestral Pueblo.

The catclaw acacia sends out roots to find water. It has dark branches and leaves. This acacia gets its name from the tiny barbs on its leaves that look like little cat claws.

Apache plume is a flowering shrub common in the desert scrub of these life zones. It can grow up to five feet (two meters) tall. Mormon tea is another shrub found here. It has needlelike stems that point skyward. Full-grown plants remain unchanged for as long as five hundred years. Mormon pioneers and American Indians used the plant's stems to make a medicinal tea.

The desert scrub is also filled with cactus-like plants. The narrowleaf yucca has spikes that are three feet (ninety-one centimeters) long with rough, sandpapery sides. The banana yucca usually blooms every year. American Indians used the strong fibers in yucca leaves to make sandals, baskets, and rope.

Dedicated to exploring the Southwest, **DesertUSA: The Guide to the American Southwest & Desert Regions** is full of resources covering subjects such as desert plants, animals, wildflowers, rivers, and geology. Pictures, maps, videos, and sections on parks and monuments are included.

Juniper and pinyon trees grow in the higher elevations of the Upper Sonoran zone. Area junipers have scraggy bark with tiny leaves and gnarled branches. Their cones look like blueberries. Pinyon pines often sprout near junipers. Their seeds, or nuts, hidden within the sticky cones, has been a popular food for centuries.

⮕ SPIDERS, INSECTS, AND BATS

Many spiders live in the Sonoran life zones. Black widows weave webs in the crevices of the Redwall Limestone. Female black widows have a red hourglass-shaped mark under their abdomen. They are poisonous.

Tarantulas live here, too. These large, hairy spiders hunt their prey on the ground instead of spinning webs.

Insects are also abundant in the Sonoran zones. Some of the most common are orange paper wasps, honey bees, black flies, and butterflies.

The insects are a source of food for many of the creatures that inhabit these zones. One, the collared lizard, grows to fourteen inches (thirty-six centimeters) long. It is tan with blue, green, and yellow markings. It has two black bands across its shoulders that look like a collar.

Canyon bats also depend on the area insects. They eat as many as five hundred insects an hour. The Western pipistrelle bat is the most common bat in GCNP. It lives in the caves of the Inner Canyon. This gray mammal has black wings with an eight-inch (twenty-centimeter) wingspan.

→ PEREGRINE FALCONS

About thirty different kinds of birds inhabit the Sonoran life zones. One, the peregrine falcon, lives in canyon cliffs. These gray and black birds have a white head and pointed wings.

Peregrines have a 43-inch (109-centimeter) wingspan. They eat other birds and bats that they hunt from above. When a peregrine sees prey, it dives at it, plucking it out of the air. Peregrines can dive up to 200 miles (322 kilometers) per hour.

During the 1960s, peregrine populations declined. This was mostly due to a chemical called DDT, which was being used to control insects in farm fields. But animals also ingested DDT as they ate and drank their food and water. The chemical made birds' eggshells thin. Many eggs broke before the babies hatched. This caused several bird populations to drop, including the peregrine. In 1973 the American peregrine was listed as an endangered animal.

DDT was banned soon after. Populations all across the United States began to rebuild. GCNP peregrines had an added advantage. Glen Canyon

Falcon Research Group - Windows Internet Explorer

http://frg.org/

Google

Falcon Research Group

Page ▾ Tools ▾

Falcon Research Group

FRG Info   Resources   Field Research   Education   Galleries   Site Map

LATEST FRG NEWS:
25 Sept. 2008 —

CURRENT PROJECTS:
SOUTHERN CROSS
PEREGRINE PROJECT:
The 2008 Southern
Migration has begun.
Read more on the
SCPP blo

—Elizabe

Done

Welcome to the Falcon Research Group (FRG) ...

The Southern Cross Peregrine Project (SCPP)

- 2008 Fall Migration -

Falcon Research Group

Grand Canyon National Park has the greatest concentration of peregrine falcons in the United States. This nonprofit group supports falcons through research, education, and conservation efforts. Its Web site features notes on field projects, photo galleries, and links to other falcon-related sites.

Access this Web site from http://www.myreportlinks.com

Dam had increased the number of birds and bats in the area. This gave the recovering peregrines an abundant food supply.

Park biologists estimate that about one hundred pairs of peregrine falcons now live in GCNP.[1] It's the largest peregrine population in the continental United States.

➔TRANSITION AND BOREAL ZONES

Just above the Upper Sonoran Zone lies the Transition Zone. It stretches from elevations of 7,000 to 8,000 feet (2,134 to 2,438 meters). The Boreal Zone is even higher. It starts at 8,000 feet (2,438 meters) and climbs to 9,000 feet (2,743 meters).

The Boreal Zone exists in the Grand Canyon area only on the North Rim.

⇒ PONDEROSA GROVES

Ponderosa pines grow in the Transition Zone of both rims. These trees can be 160 feet (49 meters) tall. They have rough, reddish bark that looks like giant puzzle pieces. Their long needles grow in clusters of three.

Quaking aspen trees grow among the ponderosas, but are much more common on the North Rim. Aspens have white bark and round green leaves that turn yellow in the fall.

Big sagebrush is also found on the rims. This gray-green plant grows to four feet (one meter). Its fragrant leaves have three tiny teeth on the end.

Wildflowers grow here, too. Among them are lupine with its rows of little purple blooms and Indian paintbrush with its red-tipped leaves.

⇒ ANIMALS OF THE RIMS

The Abert's squirrel and the Kaibab squirrel only live in ponderosa groves. These two animals are a lot alike, since they are subspecies of the same species. They are both about twenty inches (fifty centimeters) long and have tufted ears.

However, the squirrels have differences. The Abert's has a reddish back with a gray tail. It lives on the South Rim. On the other hand, the Kaibab is almost completely gray, with a reddish-colored back, but with a silver tail. It lives only one place in the world—on the North Rim of the Grand Canyon.

Actually, scientists think the Kaibab and Abert's were once the same species. They think that when the river cut through the Colorado Plateau, the squirrels on each rim slowly developed differences. These helped them live in slightly different environments.[2]

A variety of snakes and lizards also live among the ponderosas. The mountain short-horned lizard is particularly abundant.

▲ *Grand Canyon National Park has the largest population of peregrine falcons in the United States.*

Elk sightings are common on the South Rim. These thousand-pound (454-kilogram) animals have a tan body with a dark brown head and neck. They stand five feet (two meters) high at their shoulders.

Bull, or male, elk grow antlers that can weigh forty pounds (eighteen kilograms) and spread to more than five feet (two meters). Elk eat grasses, twigs, and shrubs.

Mule deer live on both rims. These grayish-brown animals have large ears. They are about three feet (ninety-one centimeters) high at the shoulder. Mule deer mostly eat brush. They summer on the canyon rims, then are likely to move into the Inner Canyon for the winter. They live in all areas of GCNP.

Bighorn sheep can also be found at all elevation levels of the canyon. Bighorn are also about three feet (ninety-one centimeters) in height. They are a light brown with a white rump. Male

The Kaibab squirrel is a small rodent that roams the park. The squirrels blend in well with the terrain around them.

△ *Scaling the rocky hillside, the bighorn sheep is a majestic creature.*

bighorns have curved horns that can weigh up to thirty pounds (fourteen kilograms). The females' horns are smaller and nearly straight. They, too, graze on leaves and grasses.

⊜ BIRDS OF THE RIMS

Golden eagles are common in the higher life zones. These golden-brown raptors have a wingspan greater than six feet (two meters).

California condors have been reintroduced to the area. These vultures have a bald, pink head

The mountain lion is the most dangerous predator stalking Grand Canyon National Park. Although, the odds that a human will encounter one are very low.

when mature. They have been described as the bird with a face that only a mother could love. Yet the condor's body is majestic. It is covered with black feathers. The undersides of an adult's wings display a white patch.

Condors are the largest bird species in North America. They can grow to thirty pounds (fourteen kilograms) with a wingspan of nine feet (three meters). Condors reach speeds of fifty miles per hour (eighty kilometers per hour) and stay in the air for hours.

Another bird common to the Grand Canyon region is the great horned owl. This owl has a brown body with darker brown spots and white throat feathers. It is about two feet (sixty-one centimeters) tall with a wingspan of up to five feet (two meters).

Wild turkeys live here, too. Turkeys are much more common on the North Rim. The males have bare blue heads and red waddles. Ancestral Pueblo raised them for food.

⊜HIGHER FORESTS

The highest elevations of GCNP are on the North Rim. The most common trees here are the Douglas fir and the white fir. Douglas firs can grow to 130 feet (40 meters) with a six-foot (two-meter) diameter. They have one-inch (three-centimeter) needles that grow along their branches. The branches on a Douglas fir are flexible. This helps them bend instead of break during the North Rim's snowy winters.

Mountain lions are the park's top predator. About one hundred are thought to live on the North Rim.[3] There are also some on the South Rim. This stealthy hunter is tan and grows to six feet (two meters) from head to tail. Mountain lions live alone and are rarely seen. A mountain lion's favorite foods are deer and elk.

Black bears also like the higher forests of GCNP. Yet they're very rare in the park because they like places with more water. Like mountain lions, they are seldom seen. Porcupines, coyotes, and chipmunks live here, too.

Chapter

5

Air pollution, though mild compared with other places, is one of the challenges facing the rangers at Grand Canyon National Park. This photo captures the canyon on a hazy evening.

Challenges to the Park

It took millions of years to form the Grand Canyon. It has taken humans less than three hundred years to change it. Not all of these changes have been good. Today, GCNP is struggling to overcome human-caused problems that could impact the canyon for centuries to come.

⊜ POLLUTION

One of the canyon's biggest problems is keeping air pollution to a minimum. On a clear day a person can see out over the canyon for more than 100 miles (161 kilometers). On some days, though, a dusty cloud hangs over the park. This haze can reduce visibility to less than fifty miles (eighty kilometers).

The pollution comes from many places. The first is lingering smoke from burning wood. The second is cars, from nearby and faraway places. In the summer, more than 6,500 cars enter the South Rim every day. Each one emits pollutants. Also, nearby downwind cities such as Phoenix, Los Angeles, and Las Vegas contribute to the pollution around GCNP.

In an effort to lessen air pollution and reduce congestion, park officials have closed some park roads to cars. Free buses service these areas, taking people to various sites. Park administrators are considering plans that include closing more roads to cars and increasing bus service.

Some park pollution comes from nearby power plants. Recent laws have made them cut the pollutants they put into the air. However, several companies have plans to build coal-fired power plants in the region. Many environmental groups are fighting to stop them. At the very least, opponents are pressuring the plants to install scrubbers to decrease toxic emissions.[1]

Grand Canyon Trust

The Grand Canyon faces challenges including pollution, forest fires, and climate change. The Grand Canyon Trust is a nonprofit group that supports the park. Its Web site describes its efforts in areas such as air quality and energy, forests, landscape protection, restoration, and water quality.

EDITOR'S CHOICE

Access this Web site from http://www.myreportlinks.com

Noise pollution also plagues the park. Planes and helicopters make more than a hundred thousand flights over the canyon every year.[2] Their engines are loud enough to drown out the park's quiet natural sounds. This disturbs tourists in the wilderness areas as well as animals. Most visitors in the developed areas of the park don't even notice them.

Laws have been made to limit flights over the Grand Canyon. Yet many people think these regulations are not enough. They believe there are still too many planes disturbing GCNP's peace. They want to limit planes even more or require aircraft that make less noise.

FIRE

Another problem in the park is forest fire. GCNP is a dry place and the threat of fire is nearly constant. At times lightning can strike dry wood and spark a fire. Untended campfires or careless people start others.

Forest fires can kill people and wildlife. They can destroy homes, property, animal habitats, and food.

Yet fire is not always bad. Fires help keep forests clean. They clear overcrowded trees. Thinned forests are healthier than overgrown ones.

Fires also clear deadwood on the forest floor. This reduces the amount of fuel available when fires do break out. With little fuel, small fires have less chance of becoming huge, out-of-control fires.

Fires can be helpful in other ways, too. When vegetation burns, nutrients are released into the soil. This makes a natural plant food. Some species even need fire to start new plants. So after a fire, these plants sprout. New vegetation attracts different animals into the area. Therefore, fires encourage diversity in an ecosystem.

Park officials manage fires carefully. When conditions look good, naturally started fires may be allowed to burn themselves out. That is, if they are not endangering people or threatening developed areas. Rangers sometimes even start small fires in controlled settings to clear deadwood.

▲ Tamarisk is a shrub that is not native to Grand Canyon National Park but has grown there in great abundance. Park officials often look for ways to remove nonnative species from park grounds.

Yet small blazes can easily grow into large, destructive wildfires. So when the weather is particularly dry, no campfires or grills are allowed inside the park. Any wildfires that threaten to grow out of control are put out as quickly as possible.

PLANT PROBLEMS

Another serious problem in GCNP is the invasion of nonnative plants. These are plants that do not grow there naturally. Some, like tamarisk, were brought into the area on purpose. Others arrived by way of car tires, people's shoes, or in some other unintentional way.

Some nonnative plants invade large areas of land, forcing out native plants. Tamarisk, for example, has taken over several beach areas and is pushing out native cottonwoods and willows. In addition, tamarisk plants pull salt from underground and shed it on the soil. This changes the chemistry of the earth. Many native plants cannot survive in this soil.

Park scientists agree that tamarisk needs to be removed in order for native plants to recover. Workers are removing tamarisk in the side canyons by pulling it, cutting it, and spraying it with herbicides.

CLIMATE CHANGE

Experts believe that global warming is already affecting the Grand Canyon. Area temperatures are rising.[3] This will lead to problems. First, higher temperatures will make the dry land even drier. This may cause more wildfires. In fact, wildfires have already increased across the West.[4]

In addition, higher temperatures could also change ecosystems within the park. Entire forests in the Southwest are dying because of warming temperatures. GCNP forests are at risk of the same fate.[5]

A loss of forest could leave plants and animals without habitats. Some species might die out and even face extinction.[6] Furthermore, a loss of native plants will allow nonnative plants to take over more land.[7]

National Parks Conservation Association

The Web site of the National Parks Conservation Association features slide shows, descriptions of park habitats, and details about efforts to protect wildlife in the parks. The site also includes park news and material from *National Parks* magazine.

Access this Web site from http://www.myreportlinks.com

Global warming could lead to a rise in certain illnesses. In the Southwest, recent droughts followed by heavy rains brought about an increase in the deer mouse population. These mice carry hantavirus, which causes an illness that can be deadly. Scientists predict that as the Southwest warms, outbreaks of this virus will increase.[8]

→ GLEN CANYON DAM

Another environmental issue that affects GCNP is Glen Canyon Dam. Everyone agrees that its creation has changed ecosystems within the park. But not everyone agrees whether this is good or bad.

Beaches have diminished and disappeared. In some places, further erosion could expose or destroy the evidence of earlier people.[9] Native fish have died out, and nonnative fish have taken over.

In view of this damage to the environment, some people want Glen Canyon Dam to be shut down. They want Lake Powell drained. They note that most of the water in the reservoir is not needed by area residents. Nearby Hoover Dam could provide electricity and water currently supplied by the Glen Canyon Dam.

Furthermore, they say, the dam leads to wasted water. Water from Lake Powell seeps into the sandstone below it. And thousands of gallons evaporate off the top of the lake every year.

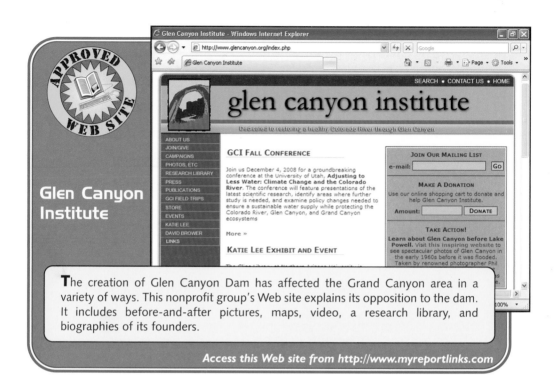

Glen Canyon Institute

The creation of Glen Canyon Dam has affected the Grand Canyon area in a variety of ways. This nonprofit group's Web site explains its opposition to the dam. It includes before-and-after pictures, maps, video, a research library, and biographies of its founders.

Access this Web site from http://www.myreportlinks.com

Finally, they argue, the dam was originally built to control flooding and insure that adequate amounts of water could be supplied to surrounding states and Mexico as required by agreements and treaties. Yet other dams such as the Hoover Dam are able to do this.

Many people, however, do not want to drain the lake. They argue that the dam has actually helped the environment. It has created food and habitats for many animals. Some of them are threatened or endangered species.

In addition, they say, shutting down Glen Canyon Dam would mean it would no longer make electricity for area residents. Some of the lost electricity would have to be made by a different power plant. This one would probably be fueled by coal, adding to area pollution and global warming.

Some of the people opposed to closing the dam are concerned about draining Lake Powell. They believe its recreational benefits outweigh the environmental concerns. Millions of people vacation at the lake every year. Not only does this provide leisure opportunities, it provides hundreds of people with jobs.

Today, people from both groups are working together. They are trying to find a compromise to the Glen Canyon Dam debate.

OVERCROWDING

More than 4 million people visit GCNP every year. Its beauty and grandeur make it one of the world's must-see sites.

Yet uninformed visitors sometimes destroy the very things they come to see. Too many people walking off park trails ruin vegetation and cause erosion. Sightseers should walk on established trails and use designated camping areas.

Furthermore, people eager to see wildlife up close sometimes feed animals. Because human-fed animals may lose the ability to find their own food, many end up starving. This can also lead to people being hurt by animals, catching diseases from the animals, and littering. GCNP visitors

▲ *Although some environmentalists oppose the Glen Canyon Dam, others support it. Those who support it are afraid that closing the dam would drain Lake Powell, shown here. Lake Powell is used by many for recreation.*

should never feed wildlife. They must be careful to pick up all food scraps and haul out trash.

All Grand Canyon visitors should follow the "leave no trace" code. This motto means that after a person visits the wilderness, there should be no trace of that visit—nothing left in the area and nothing taken from it. Some people like to say, "Take only pictures, and leave only footprints."

⮕ BUDGET

Every year, more people visit GCNP than the year before. This means that every year the park needs more money to take care of more guests. Yet the GCNP's operating budget did not increase during the early 2000s.[10]

Many other national parks have faced the same problem. In fact, some people believe that the annual National Park Service (NPS) budget is $600 million less than what the national parks need to operate.[11]

Due to this, many parks have had to rely on donations to continue some programs. In GCNP, for example, the Grand Canyon Association has donated money for trail building, controlling invasive species, and protecting the condors. Some people believe that without this money, some park programs would cease to exist.[12]

Less money also means less research. Yet research is vital to keeping the park healthy.

The **National Park Foundation** campaigns to help maintain America's national parks. The group's Web site also includes articles from its publication, *Parks* magazine, and photo and essay contests.

Scientists need to study the changing climate to understand how it will affect GCNP. They need time to develop solutions to problems warming might create. Biologists need to study plants and animals. How are endangered and threatened species doing? How do the habits and behaviors of one species affect another?

RESCUE

Visitor safety might be the biggest concern in GCNP. Nearly every year, someone falls into the canyon and dies. GCNP visitors should be careful on the rims. They should watch out for loose rocks and wind gusts.

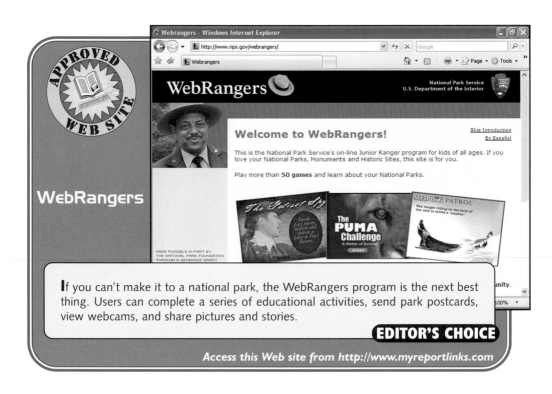

If you can't make it to a national park, the WebRangers program is the next best thing. Users can complete a series of educational activities, send park postcards, view webcams, and share pictures and stories.

EDITOR'S CHOICE

Access this Web site from http://www.myreportlinks.com

Hikers must also be careful on long hikes. Rangers assist hundreds of hikers along canyon trails every year. Many have been overcome with heat or exhaustion. Hikers should choose reasonable destinations. For example, no one should try to hike from the rim to the river and back in a day. They should not hike in the midday heat of summer. They should drink and eat regularly, use sunscreen, and wear protective clothing.

Thunderstorms pose another danger. July, August, and early September in GCNP are known for heavy afternoon rains. These are called monsoons. Monsoons often bring dangerous lightning. Visitors should move away from the rim and exposed areas and get to safety when they see lightning.

Monsoons can also cause flash, or rapid, flooding. This puts people hiking in slot canyons (canyons with steep walls) at special risk. When water rushes through these canyons, there is nowhere to climb to safety. Hikers should avoid slot canyons if rain threatens. In fact, during monsoon season the NPS discourages people from hiking the slot canyons. Wide, flat areas can also pose dangers. Hikers should always be aware of weather forecasts and keep an eye on the sky.

Yet even with its dangers, people can have safe adventures in GCNP. In fact, a well-prepared visitor can have the experience of a lifetime.

Chapter

6

Visiting the Grand Canyon

My legs were tired. My feet hurt. My knees were skinned from a tumble, and I had cactus needles in my arm. But I was happy. Thrilled, actually. I had made it—made it to the bottom of the Grand Canyon.

Mom woke us up while it was still dark outside. I wasn't tired, though. I was excited. All of Dad's training, miles and miles of walking around the track, was going to be put to the test. We'd be glad, he said. We'd be glad we were in shape when it was time to hike the canyon. And you know what? He was right!

We gulped down our breakfast and headed for the trail. It was still gray outside.

Other hikers were already there. After a quick picture and Dad's last-minute check of our backpacks, we started down. The sky looked like it had been splashed with pink and blue watercolor paint. The rocks on the horizon were glowing red and orange.

Before long, the trail turned completely around and we were hiking with the sun at our backs. After passing through a tunnel, the trail turned the other way again. Now I could see the sun peeking over the horizon. It was a fuzzy white ball.

Another tunnel made a window in the distance. We walked through it and suddenly the Grand Canyon was facing me. It looked huge!

Just inches from the trail the land dropped away. I moved closer to the wall on the other side. We walked in silence, listening to the quiet of the morning. I thought about not falling off the cliff.

WALKING THROUGH THE PAST

By now the sun had cleared the horizon and was too bright to look at. We stopped at Mile-and-a-Half Resthouse to put on our sunglasses and hats. I was a little surprised that Mile-and-a-Half Resthouse wasn't a house at all. It was just a small pavilion made of rocks and a separate restroom building.

We moved on, slowing our pace. Somewhere nearby, prehistoric American Indians had made rock paintings. Mom said that American Indians had hiked this trail centuries before miners came into the area. It was cool to think that American Indians had walked this same path so long ago. My brother saw the pictographs first. They were orange. A few looked like elk.

Now the trail got steeper. Dad reminded us to concentrate on our walking. Every once in a while we stopped to look out over the canyon. It was unbelievable. I felt like I was on another planet. The rocks were hundreds of shades of orange, red, purple, and blue. How could rocks be such colors?

Three-Mile Resthouse came up before I knew it. It looked a lot like the pavilion at Mile-and-a-Half Resthouse. Mom made us stop for drinks and an apple. "Second breakfast," she called it.

After a few steep switchbacks, the trail flattened out. Suddenly, I realized that sometime that morning the canyon had swallowed me. I was no longer above it, but inside it! Walls of rock surrounded me

Created by a photographer, **Grand Canyon Explorer** is well thought out and presents abundant information for planning a visit and getting to know the Grand Canyon's north and south rims. Each section has numerous links to other Web resources.

EDITOR'S CHOICE

and I was amongst stone towers I had once looked down on.

The oasis of green in front of me interrupted my thoughts. We were coming up on Indian Garden. As we got closer, I tripped on a rock and landed on a prickly pear cactus. It was definitely prickly.

We found a shady spot under a cottonwood tree and sat down. Dad took out the first aid kit and pulled needles from my hand. I recited multiplication facts to take my mind off the pain. It felt better when he was done and had sprayed my hand with medicine.

We sat in the shade eating trail mix and noticing the plants around us. Then we refilled our

"The Canyon" is a travel and informational Web site providing extensive news and data about Grand Canyon National Park. It may be helpful when planning a trip.

Access this Web site from http://www.myreportlinks.com

water bottles and headed back to the trail. We still had a long way to go.

Dad told us we were really walking back in time. Each footstep, he said, took us thousands of years into the earth's past.[1] Thinking about that made the minutes go by quickly.

It was now mid-morning and the air was getting hot. Luckily, the trail followed the creek. Every once in a while, a cool breeze came off the water and drifted over us—until we started down the Devil's Corkscrew. Here the trail zigzagged through black rocks. Heat bounced off the stone and I felt like I was baking.

➔ THE *ROLLING* COLORADO

Just when I thought I couldn't stand it anymore, I heard a roaring sound. And then there it was—the Colorado River! Depending on how the sun was shining, the water seemed to change color with every step I took. First it was brown, then yellow, then green.

We found a little beach where we took off our shoes and socks and waded into the water. It was wonderfully cold! I splashed myself all over, and then found a good sitting rock and opened my lunch bag.

After eating, I was ready for the last few miles of our hike. We followed the river to the Bright

Angel Suspension Bridge, or, as most hikers call it, the Silver Bridge.

It looked scary. It was so high above the water—and narrow. The thin cables that held it up didn't look very sturdy. But Mom said millions of hikers had used the bridge, and it was plenty strong enough.

Dad went first and then my brother. I was next. I took a deep breath and stepped onto the bridge. Mom followed. She told me not to look down. But halfway across, I couldn't resist. The river was far, far below me. I felt dizzy and stopped for a minute. Mom spoke softly and told me to keep walking. Once my feet began to move, I didn't look down again. And then I was across.

The last part of the hike went fast. Before long we were at Phantom Ranch. Our tiny cabin was behind it.

My hand still hurt a little and my feet hurt a lot. But I had made it! I had hiked almost ten miles! My brother and I laughed about

◀ A hiker stares out over the vast expanse of Grand Canyon National Park.

nothing as we plopped onto the beds. I didn't want to get up for hours.

Tonight we'll look at the stars from inside the Grand Canyon. Tomorrow we'll play in a creek and explore a side canyon. And then comes the real work—hiking back up!

➡ HIKING, BIKING, AND SKIING

More than fifty thousand people hike to the bottom of the Grand Canyon every year. Many spend a night or two there. A few hardy trekkers hike from one rim to the other in a day. This rim-to-rim hike is about twenty-one miles (thirty-four kilometers) long, depending on which trails the hikers use. Still, the NPS encourages hikers not to attempt this. They think it's best for people to stop and rest for a night.

Some people prefer to get to the bottom of the canyon by mule. A variety of mule trips are available from either rim, but North Rim trips are all day trips that go only partway down the North Kaibab Trail. Trips range from a few hours to several days in length. All rides must be reserved well in advance.

Some hikers add to their fun by fishing. The Colorado River holds several great fishing holes. One of the best places is just upstream from Phantom Ranch. An Arizona fishing license is required

Billed as "the most complete Grand Canyon National Park travel guide," **Grand Canyon National Park: TravelWest** has numerous sections, a photo and video gallery, coverage of park history and weather, and links to other parks in the area and nearby cities.

to fish in the park. All anglers should be aware of regulations regarding catch limits and lures.

Of course, the trails to the bottom aren't the only trails in the park. GCNP has 38 trails that cover 400 miles (644 kilometers) of land. Some wind through meadows and forests. Others skirt the rims. A few trails are even used for bicycling.

⊖ Rafting the Colorado River

One of the most adventurous ways to see the Grand Canyon is by river. Many different kinds of boats run the Colorado every year. A motorized raft can travel the entire length in about a week. People-powered crafts are slower. But rafts, kayaks, and dories allow paddlers to see the river at its natural pace.

Boaters camp overnight on riverside beaches. Many spend an extra day or two hiking through side canyons to ruins and waterfalls.

River runners should be well prepared for the trip. Many rapids are dangerous even for an experienced rafter.

Sixteen concessioners are approved to offer guided river trips that range from one day to several days. All river runners need a permit from GCNP. Only a certain amount of permits are given out in a lottery system. Many people wait years to win reservations to raft the river.

SCENIC DRIVES

The most popular way to see the canyon is by car. North Rim roads are closed during winter months due to snow. The South Rim, however, is accessible all year.

A family driving to the South Rim in the summer may have difficulty finding a parking spot at some overlooks. For this reason, many people choose to ride a shuttle bus. A leisurely day can be spent hopping from one viewpoint to another. An evening ride to Hermits Rest to watch the sunset ends the day with a spectacular light show.

→ EDUCATION

GCNP offers many learning opportunities. The Grand Canyon Field Institute, for example, is a nonprofit organization that leads backpacking trips and other outings. Participants learn about park paleontology, ecology, and archaeology through hands-on adventures.

In addition, free ranger talks are given every day at several different sites. All offer fascinating information about the canyon. For example, one talk is given at a fossil bed. Here visitors can actually see and touch the fossilized marine creatures that lived before the dinosaurs. Another talk available during some seasons, called "Way Cool Stuff for Kids," features games and activities related to the canyon. Moon walks and star talks take on the canyon at night.

▲ The view from the South Rim Overlook. Many opt to take a scenic drive through Grand Canyon National Park, stopping at every overlook where they can get a parking space.

A close inspection of Grand Canyon Village is really a lesson in history. This entire area has been declared a National Historic Landmark District. It holds more than two hundred historic buildings. Many are open to tourists.

⇒ LODGING

For those able to spend more than a day at GCNP, the South Rim has several lodging options. A stay in the historic El Tovar Hotel gives visitors a flavor of the canyon's early days. Nearby Bright Angel Lodge contains a fireplace made from canyon rocks. Its layers are stacked in the same order as they occur in the canyon.[2]

One of the most luxurious guest suites in the park is the O'Neill Cabin. Buckey O'Neill, who lived in Grand Canyon Village in the 1890s, is likely to have occupied this building. The building has been preserved and can now be rented by guests as part of the Bright Angel Lodge. The South Rim has two campgrounds and Trailer Village for RVs. One remains open year-round.

The North Rim has fewer places to house overnight guests. Grand Canyon Lodge offers motel-type rooms and small cabins to rent. The North Rim Campground has many sites for tents and RVs. Far to the west is Tuweep Campground. It is a primitive facility.

The Inner Canyon also has limited lodging. There are a few campgrounds, like Indian Garden Campground, along trails to the bottom. At the canyon bottom is Bright Angel Campground. Also at the bottom is Phantom Ranch, with its cabins and hiker dormitories. In most cases, hikers headed to any of these places need reservations and backcountry permits.

Some people enjoy camping in undeveloped areas. These backpackers hike to places all over GCNP to enjoy the solitude of the wilderness. Backcountry campers need backpacking permits.

HAVASU FALLS

Havasupai Indian Reservation is in a side canyon on the south side of the Colorado River. It is not a part of the park. It belongs to and is governed by the Havasupai Tribe.

Supai is the only town on the reservation. It is home to about 450 Havasupai. There are only two ways to get to Supai. One is an eight-mile (thirteen-kilometer) trail from Hualapai Hilltop. The other is by helicopter.

A trail from Supai leads to what have been called "some of the prettiest waterfalls on earth."[3] The 75-foot (23-meter) Navajo Falls and 150-foot (46-meter) Havasu Falls are just a few miles from town. The granddaddy of all of the parks falls, two hundred-foot (sixty-one-meter) Mooney Falls, is a ten-mile (sixteen-kilometer) hike from Hualapai Hilltop.

Each waterfall is more stunning than the one before it. Havasu Falls is the most visited. Its sparkling white waters come streaming over a high stone ledge. Bright red rock borders the falls. A sapphire sky sweeps over it. The falling water seems suspended in the air until it hits the pool below. There it creates a frothy cauldron of white water.

As the waters calm, they change from white to an incredible bluish-green. The turquoise color is striking. Sand lines the water. Beyond the little beaches are bright-green cottonwood trees. These falls make evident the reason for the native people's name, for the Havasupai are known as the "people of the blue-green water."

➔ HUALAPAI RESERVATION

The Hualapai Indian Reservation is also on

Havasu Falls is located within the Havasupai Indian Reservation in Grand Canyon National Park. Havasu Falls is a popular tourist destination.

the south side of the river. It covers rugged canyons as well as the grasslands and forests of the rim. The Hualapai are called the "people of the tall pine."

About 1,500 tribe members live on the Hualapai Reservation. Many are ranchers. Others tend the tourist trade. They guide river tours and hunting trips, make and sell art, and work at Grand Canyon West.

Grand Canyon West is a tourist attraction. It offers several activities, such as the Old West town that lets visitors feel as if they are stepping back in time. Indian Village includes life-sized models of American Indian homes from several tribes.

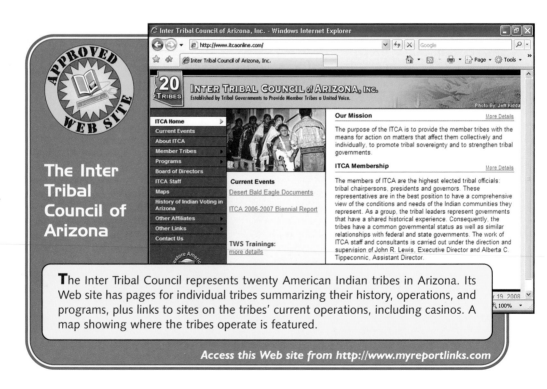

The Inter Tribal Council of Arizona

The Inter Tribal Council represents twenty American Indian tribes in Arizona. Its Web site has pages for individual tribes summarizing their history, operations, and programs, plus links to sites on the tribes' current operations, including casinos. A map showing where the tribes operate is featured.

Access this Web site from http://www.myreportlinks.com

The jewel of Grand Canyon West is the skywalk. This horseshoe-shaped bridge extends out over a deep side canyon. Its walls and floor are made of a special kind of glass. Those who are brave enough to walk out onto the bridge can look straight down into the canyon's abyss.

TUSAYAN

The tiny town of Tusayan sits just a mile from GCNP's south entrance. It is home to just six hundred people. But a large *National Geographic* visitor center is here. It is a great place for tourists heading to the park to stop for information about lodging, attractions, and events. The center's Grand Canyon IMAX Theater plays an informative and thrilling movie about the canyon. Tusayan also offers several hotels and restaurants.

WILLIAMS

Williams is sixty miles (ninety-seven kilometers) south of the South Rim. A train regularly runs from Williams to Grand Canyon Village just as it did in the early 1900s. The train's cars have been restored to look as they did in 1923. Tickets for this ride are purchased in a 1908 hotel. Every summer morning, a Wild West shoot-out is staged for tourists in front of this hotel. Williams also has several other hotels and many restaurants for Grand Canyon visitors.

→FLAGSTAFF

Flagstaff is 90 miles (145 kilometers) from GCNP. This city of fifty-five thousand people has its own sightseeing opportunities. North of Flagstaff is Sunset Crater Volcano National Monument. Sunset Crater was made during a series of volcanic eruptions around the year 1100. A trail there winds through hardened lava flows and cinder fields.

Walnut Canyon National Monument is just east of town. It preserves several cliff dwellings and homes where Ancestral Pueblo once lived.

Offered by the Arizona Office of Tourism, **Arizona Guide** provides everything you need to plan a visit to the state and the Grand Canyon area. Maps show points of interest, scenic routes, and recreational opportunities.

Flagstaff is also full of lodges and restaurants. Outfitters here can prepare visitors for almost any Grand Canyon adventure.

THE RESERVOIRS

Outside opposite ends of GCNP are Lake Mead and Lake Powell. Both are popular recreation sites. People from near and far visit the lakes to enjoy boating, fishing, swimming, and other water activities.

THE BREATHTAKING CANYON

Seeing the Grand Canyon is an unforgettable experience. A first view can even be somewhat shocking. From a distance, soft green land and dense forests stretch out as far as the eye can see. There is no sign of any chasm, no hint of a great gaping hole in the earth. Then, suddenly, the earth seems to yawn and the Grand Canyon opens. Without warning an unbelievable landscape appears. Walls of red, orange, brown, and even blue-gray rocks take over the earth. Stone towers and rock temples rise from unseen depths. And between them all is space. Space that is so wide and empty that the mind has a hard time taking it all in.

That's when you know: You are at the Grand Canyon.

Report Links

The Internet sites described below can be accessed at
http://www.myreportlinks.com

▶ **Grand Canyon National Park**
Editor's Choice Learn all about the Grand Canyon, and plan a visit to the North or South rim.

▶ **Grand Canyon National Park: Oh, Ranger!**
Editor's Choice You study up on the Grand Canyon and plan a trip by using this Oh, Ranger! Web site.

▶ **Grand Canyon Explorer**
Editor's Choice Find out about hiking, backpacking, and other fun activities in Grand Canyon area.

▶ **Grand Canyon Trust**
Editor's Choice The Grand Canyon Trust tries to improve the conditions at Grand Canyon National Park.

▶ **The Flora**
Editor's Choice Read about the different types of plant life that are found in the Canyon's five life zone

▶ **WebRangers**
Editor's Choice With the WebRangers program, you can become a virtual National Park ranger!

▶ **The Anasazi or "Ancient Pueblo"**
Learn about the Anasazi, longtime inhabitants of the Colorado Plateau.

▶ **Arizona Guide**
Find out about fun activities for visitors anywhere in the state of Arizona.

▶ **Arizona Maps (Perry-Castaneda Library Map Collection)**
Use this collection of maps to learn about the geography of the Grand Canyon and the state of Arizona.

▶ **California Condor (U.S. Fish and Wildlife Service)**
Discover efforts to preserve the California Condor and other endangered species in the Grand Canyon.

▶ **DesertUSA: The Guide to the American Southwest & Desert Regions**
A guide to the desert habitat of the American Southwest.

▶ **Falcon Research Group**
This nonprofit group helps support falcons through efforts in research, education, and conservation.

▶ **The Geology of the Grand Canyon**
Read about each layer of the Grand Canyon, from its core to its surface, and how the layers formed.

▶ **Glen Canyon Institute**
Research the controversy over Glen Canyon Dam, and see its effect on the Grand Canyon.

▶ **Grand Canyon Lodging**
See where you can stay overnight in Grand Canyon National Park.

The Internet sites described below can be accessed at

http://www.myreportlinks.com

▶ **Grand Canyon National Park: TravelWest**
Read about hiking, biking, skiing, rafting and other activities you can take part in on your visit there.

▶ **Grand Canyon National Park Service**
"The Canyon" Web site aims to give you all you need for a trip to GCNP.

▶ **Grand Canyon Railway**
It's never too late to take a vintage train to Grand Canyon National Park! Find out how, here.

▶ **Havasupai Indian Reservation**
Learn about an American Indian group that was temporarily displaced by GCNP.

▶ **The Inter Tribal Council of Arizona**
Get to know the history of twenty American Indian tribes in the vicinity of the Grand Canyon.

▶ **John Muir Exhibit**
John Muir founded the Sierra Club and influenced the development of America's national parks.

▶ **John Wesley Powell Memorial Museum**
Exhibits about the life and times of one of the early explorers of the Rocky Mountain area.

▶ *The Journey of Coronado, 1540–1542*
A first-person account of the travels of explorer Francisco Coronado.

▶ **Living Rivers: Colorado Riverkeeper**
Read about the impact of Glen Canyon Dam, and the controversy it has caused.

▶ **Missions Initiative (Arizona State Museum)**
Learn about the historic role of Spanish colonial missions, and preservation efforts.

▶ **Museum of Northern Arizona**
Discover the heritage, culture, lands, and peoples of the Colorado Plateau.

▶ **National Park Foundation**
The National Park Foundation helps preserve the U.S. national parks.

▶ **National Parks Conservation Association**
This group helps protect the habitats and wildlife of U.S. national parks.

▶ **National Park Service**
Explore America's national parks through interactive presentations.

▶ **Treaty of Guadalupe Hidalgo**
Find out how the United States acquired the Grand Canyon area after the Mexican-American War.

Ancestral Pueblo—American Indians who lived in the southwestern United States from A.D. 1 to 1300. They are sometimes referred to as Ancient Pueblo or the Anasazi.

archaeologist—A scientist who studies human cultures through material remains.

artifact—A human-made object of historical interest.

burro—A donkey used for carrying goods and people.

climate change—Changes in modern climate including the rise in temperatures often referred to as global warming.

desert scrub—A area dotted with very small trees or shrubs.

erosion—The movement or wearing away of soil, mud, and rocks by water and wind.

fossil—The remains or evidence of animals or plants that have been preserved in rock.

geology—The study of the history of the earth focusing on what can be learned from rocks.

Great Depression—A worldwide decline in business that started in 1929 and lasted until the start of World War II. During the Great Depression, many Americans were unemployed and lived in poverty.

Indian Reservation—An area of land set aside for American Indians by the United States government during the period of Westward Expansion. Many American Indians were made to move from their homelands during this time and forced to live in a specific area.

kiva—A room used by Pueblo Indians for religious or social purposes.

monsoons—Heavy rains or a rainy season.

Mormon—A member of the Church of Jesus Christ of Latter-day Saints.

native—Something that occurs in an area naturally or has been there for a long time (plants, animals, or people).

paleontologist—A person who studies prehistoric life forms by examining fossils.

pictograph—A symbol or picture painted on stone using mineral dyes.

plateau—An area of high land that is relatively flat.

rapids—A section of river where the current runs swiftly over a rocky bed.

reservoir—A man-made lake used to store water.

switchback—A sharp turn that allows a trail to move gradually up or down a steep hill.

tributaries—Streams that break off from a river and feed into either a larger stream or a lake.

Chapter 1. Mountain Lying Down

1. APN Media, LLC, "Grand Canyon National Park: History," *American Park Network,* 2008, <http://www .americanparknetwork.com/parkinfo/content.asp?catid=85&cont enttypeid=43> (August 8, 2008).

2. National Park Service, "Weather," *Grand Canyon National Park,* January 17, 2007, <http://www.nps.gov/grca /naturescience/weather.htm> (August 8, 2008).

3. Allyson Mathis and Carl Bowman, "The Grand Age of Rocks: The Numeric Ages for Rocks Exposed Within Grand Canyon," *National Park Service Nature and Science,* 2006, <http://www2.nature.nps.gov/geology/parks/grca/age/index .cfm> (August 8, 2008).

Chapter 2. The Making of the Canyon

1. Tom Pittenger, National Park Service spokesperson for Grand Canyon National Park, comments on manuscript, January 2008.

2. National Park Service, "Ranger Minute: How Old," *Grand Canyon National Park,* May 19, 2008, <http://www.nps.gov /grca/photosmultimedia/rangermin200703howold_wmv.htm> (August 8, 2008).

3. Living Rivers, "Grand Canyon & Glen Canyon Dam: The Basics," *Grand Canyon Campaign,* August 6, 2004, <http ://www.savegrandcanyon.org/campaigns/grandcanyon/article1 .cfm> (August 8, 2008).

4. Scott A. Elias, *The Ice-Age History of Southwestern National Parks* (Washington, D.C.: Smithsonian Institution Press, 1997), p. 120.

5. "American Indians at Grand Canyon—Past and Present," *Grandcanyon.com,* 1995–2008, <http://www.grandcanyon.com /american-indians.html> (August 8, 2008).

6. Seymour L. Fishbein, *Grand Canyon Country: Its Majesty and Its Lore* (Washington, D.C.: National Geographic Society, 1997), p. 19.

7. Edward Dolnick, *Down the Great Unknown* (New York: Harper Collins, 2001), p. 15.

8. "Major John Wesley Powell," *John Wesley Powell Memorial Museum,* n.d., <http://www.powellmuseum.org/MajorPowell .html> (August 8, 2008).

9. National Park Service, "Scenic Vistas," *Grand Canyon National Park,* January 17, 2007, <http://home.nps.gov/grca/ naturescience/scenicvistas.htm> (August 8, 2008).

10. APN Media, LLC, "Grand Canyon National Park: History," *American Park Network,* 2008, <http://www.americanparknetwork .com/parkinfo/content.asp?catid=85&contenttypeid=43> (August 8, 2008).

11. ABOR/Northern Arizona University, "Hualapai Historical Events," *Indigenous Voices of the Colorado Plateau,* 2005, <http://library.nau.edu/speccoll/exhibits/indigenous_voices/hualapai/events.html> (August 8, 2008).

12. National Park Service, "Forests," *Grand Canyon National Park,* January 18, 2007, <http://www.nps.gov/grca/naturescience/forests.htm> (August 11, 2008).

13. "Grand Canyon National Park," *National Geographic,* 1996–2008, <http://www.nationalgeographic.com/destinations/Grand_Canyon_National_Park> (August 11, 2008).

Chapter 3. The New Park

1. Michael F. Anderson, ed., *Polishing the Jewel: An Administrative History of Grand Canyon National Park* (Grand Canyon, Ariz.: Grand Canyon Association, 2000), p. 20.

2. Brad Dimock, "Glen Rollin Hyde" and "Bessie Louise Haley Hyde," *The Charley Project,* November 15, 2005, <http://www.charleyproject.org/cases/h/hyde_glen.html> and <http://www.charleyproject.org/cases/h/hyde_bessie.html> (August 11, 2008).

3. Living Rivers, "Grand Canyon & Glen Canyon Dam: The Basics," *Grand Canyon Campaign,* August 6, 2004, <http://www.livingrivers.org/campaigns/grandcanyon/article1.cfm> (August 11, 2008).

4. Havasu Baaja', "About Us," *Havasupai Tribe,* n.d., <http://www.havasupaitribe.com/aboutus.html> (August 11, 2008).

5. J. Donald Hughes, "Scenery Versus Habitat at the Grand Canyon," in Michael F. Anderson, *A Gathering of Grand Canyon Historians: Ideas, Arguments, and First-Person Accounts* (Grand Canyon, Ariz.: Grand Canyon Association, 2005), p. 108.

6. National Park Service, "Places to Go," *Grand Canyon National Park,* May 23, 2008, <http://www.nps.gov/grca/planyourvisit/placestogo.htm> (August 11, 2008).

7. Seymour L. Fishbein, *Grand Canyon Country: Its Majesty and Its Lore* (Washington, D.C.: National Geographic Society, 1997), p. 139.

Chapter 4. Plant and Animal Life

1. National Park Service, "Birds," *Grand Canyon National Park,* June 25, 2008, <http://www.nps.gov/grca/naturescience/birds.htm> (August 11, 2008).

2. National Park Service, "Kaibab Squirrel," *Views of the National Parks,* n.d., <http://www.nature.nps.gov/views/Sites/PARA/HTML/ET_05_Ecology.htm> (August 11, 2008).

3. Shane Christensen, *Grand Canyon National Park* (Hoboken, N.J.: Wiley Publishing, Inc., 2004), p. 189.

Chapter 5. Challenges to the Park

1. National Park Service, "Environmental Factors," *Grand Canyon National Park,* September 10, 2008, <http://www.nps.gov/grca/naturescience/environmentalfactors.htm> (September 11, 2008).

2. "Meeting the Natives," *Nature: Grand Canyon,* n.d., <http://www.pbs.org/wnet/nature/grandcanyon/natives.html> (August 11, 2008).

3. Stephen Saunders and Maureen Maxwell, "Less Snow, Less Water: Climate Disruption in the West," *The Rocky Mountain Climate Association,* September 2005, <http://www.rockymountainclimate.org/website%20pictures/Less%20Snow%20Less%20Water.pdf> (August 11, 2008).

4. Ibid.

5. Stephen Saunders and Tom Easley, "Losing Ground: Western National Parks Endangered by Climate Disruption," *National Resources Defense Council,* July 2006, <http://www.nrdc.org/land/parks/gw/contents.asp> (August 11, 2008).

6. Ibid., pp. 6–9.

7. Ibid., p. 9.

8. World Resources Institute, "Expected Impacts of Global Warming," *Climate Protection and the National Interest,* 1997, <http://archive.wri.org/page.cfm?id=2149&z=?> (August 11, 2008)

9. Seymour L. Fishbein, *Grand Canyon Country: Its Majesty and Its Lore* (Washington, D.C.: National Geographic Society, 1997), p. 20.

10 Lee Davidson, "National Parks in Budget Turmoil," *Desert Morning News*, September 26, 2004, <http://deseretnews.com/article/1,5143,595093817,00.html> (August 11, 2008).

11. Geotimes, "Funding: National Parks in Crisis," December 2005, <http://www.agiweb.org/geotimes/dec05/NN_NPS.html> (August 11, 2008).

12. Ibid.

Chapter 6. Visiting the Grand Canyon

1. Donald L. Baars, *The Colorado Plateau* (Albuquerque: University of New Mexico Press, 2000), p. 4.

2. Shane Christensen, *Grand Canyon National Park* (Hoboken, N.J.: Wiley Publishing, Inc., 2004), p. 55.

3. Ibid., p. 161.

Beckman, Wendy Hart. *National Parks in Crisis: Debating the Issues.* Berkeley Heights, N.J.: Enslow Publishers, Inc., 2004.

Fitzpatrick, Anne. *Grand Canyon.* Mankato, Minn.: Creative Education, 2005.

Halvorsen, Lisa. *Grand Canyon.* Woodbridge, Conn.: Blackbirch Press, 2000.

Hamilton, John. *Grand Canyon National Park.* Edina, Minn.: ABDO Publishing Co., 2005.

Kallen, Stuart A. *The Grand Canyon.* San Diego, Calif.: KidHaven Press, 2003.

Lindemann, Linda Lou. *Colorado River Briefs for a Trip Through the Grand Canyon.* Page, Ariz.: L.L. Lindemann, 2005.

Petersen, David. *Grand Canyon National Park.* New York: Children's Press, 2001.

Roop, Connie and Peter, eds. *The Diary of John Wesley Powell: Conquering the Grand Canyon.* New York: Benchmark Books, 2001.

Schlesinger, Jr., Arthur M., and Fred L. Israel, eds. *Grand Canyon Experiences: Chronicles From National Geographic.* Philadelphia: Chelsea House Publishers, 2000.

Temple, Teri and Bob. *Welcome to Grand Canyon National Park.* Chanhassen, Minn.: Child's World, 2006.